Thoughts

Life of a Suicide

Dillan Kane

authorHOUSE®

AuthorHouse™
1663 Liberty Drive, Suite 200
Bloomington, IN 47403
www.authorhouse.com
Phone: 1-800-839-8640

First published by AuthorHouse 1/19/2009

ISBN: 978-1-4389-2186-0 (sc)

Printed in the United States of America
Bloomington, Indiana

This book is printed on acid-free paper.

Introduction

Goodnight Jason, Grandpa, Grandma, Grandpa, Grandma, Goodnight Kate, Barb, Rick, John, Dick, Glen, Goodnight, Goodnight Dad. Goodnight to those that have passed on, in my life. This is how I end the day each night before going to bed. It is something that I do for myself to give appreciation to the people in my life now and in the past. Sometimes I just say the words, but they give me comfort in feeling the energy of the people of my past and how they are still in my life in some way, and more appreciation for the people here with me now. As time goes on the list gets longer, with the reality coming closer, that death is just a part of life. Death is full of mystery and the unknown. It is based on beliefs, hopes and faith. Death means different things based on how you define it. This is my attempt to define it and understand it for myself. This is also my attempt to understand the impulses of suicide. These are my thoughts and the thoughts that can help create the groundwork of a suicide. Thoughts create the story, so being able to step back from the story and see what story you are creating whether here or there. Being able to step back and recognizing your more than your story, being able to stop the story when you need and want to, and change the story, so healing can take place. Recognizing your having the thoughts, but your more than your thoughts, the good and bad. Thoughts don't have to be taken to action, only looked at, and taken for what they are, passing into other thoughts. Not defining who you are and where you are to go. With depression that leads to suicidal thoughts you can become lost in your own thoughts, lost in defining what one is perceiving and how it affects you and what you want.

This is also a story about the other core idea or question of what may happen if life didn't end at physical death. What would be the life of a suicide that continues even after one takes their own life? Everyone will eventually come face to face with death and what that may bring.

COMMONALITIES OF SUICIDE
By Edwin Shneidman

10 Commonalities of Suicide are as follows:
The common purpose of suicide is to seek a solution.
The common goal of suicide is cessation of consciousness.
The common stimulus of suicide is unbearable psychological pain.
The common stressor in suicide is frustrated psychological needs.
The common emotion in suicide is hopelessness.
The common cognitive state in suicide is ambivalence.
The common perceptual state in suicide is constriction.
The common action in suicide is escape.
The common interpersonal act in suicide is communication of intention.
The common pattern in suicide is consistency of lifelong styles

These are the commonalities or thoughts that I use to help understand the process of suicide and how life can be perceived by a person in suicidal ideation. There is really no box you can put suicide in to explain every situation, it's a combination of many different things. This is just a start of understanding the "why". It is just not the thoughts but the story that is created. Thoughts are fueled by emotions, experiences and at times a mind and body that is out of balance or ill at times. Being able to stop and step back and see how your thoughts and stories are unfolding and recognize if is not where you want to be or is not working for you. Recognizing it is okay to ask for and accept help so you can accept what you are experiencing so you can change it. To get the support you need, whether it is only for that moment that is clouded with emotions of suicide, which can change with storms of the wind. It is never too late. These are just some of the common themes that are generated. Beneath these core commonalties are the events and stories of individual life's. It doesn't depict the full, sometimes daily struggles that a person can have.

Chapter of Thoughts

The Ending of a Life   1

Talking to Someone   25

Working Out the Issues   40

Hindsight with Suicide   52

Working in the Mental Health System   60

Depression, Mental Illness, and ADHD   80

Looking for a Missing Person   87

Conclusions So Far   104

Dancing with Death   122

The Ending of a Life

I started writing these thoughts after my brother Jason committed suicide in October of 1999 and have from time to time written since then, when something in my life encourages me to. The death of my Dad, has been one of those encouragements to start writing again, even if sporadically. He passed away from lung cancer after a good battle with it in his final year of his earthly life. In many ways I wished I could of shared more of my thoughts with him in that final year, so that is why I continue to put them down on paper. I did get to spend time with Dad, during those final months and days, that I will always treasure but there will be always times I will miss his physical presence in my life. Even through he had many moments of struggling with physical discomforts and pains, he had a presence of peace about himself that he portrayed to myself and others often in those last days. He always seemed to have a fight in him, even toward the end. Not the kind of fight that you know your not going to die, but the kind of fight to die with dignity and peace about the ending of a life. Doing those little things he wanted to, not necessarily doing great exciting things with grand adventure, just taking the time to enjoy what he has and could do. Taking the time to enjoy the moments. Being able to spend time with family and friends, doing things he enjoyed, spending time on his boat, spending time on the river and just being a part of life until those final moments until his body was transitioned from the physical to the spiritual.

When he was first diagnosed it wasn't a major surprise, since he was a heavy smoker for several years. You see those warning labels all the time about smoking. Most smokers know of the risk but are willing to keep smoking or just aren't able to stop. My Dad kept smoking as close to the end at his life as he could, until his body couldn't tolerate it anymore. He was only able to stop because his body couldn't tolerate it and it didn't bring any pleasure, only pain and discomfort. So I really got to understand how strong the inclination to continue to smoke was for him and for many. After being diagnosed, there was the awareness that life wouldn't be easy for him, or any of us regarding his illness. You knew the cancer was inside his body trying to gain a hold of him and take his life from him. That moment from the first cigarette he smoked to the time of being diagnosed was now only separated with a thought.

It soon had became a time to plan a course of action against the cancer. Something that would give him the best chance to beat it, if any, with some kind of quality of life while going through treatments. There was always some hope he could somehow beat it, but you knew it wasn't great. Lung cancer is a tough disease that takes what it wants and destroys. Dad decided to have chemo treatments about every 3 weeks, where he was pumped with various chemicals that would try to attack the cancer to possibly extend his life. Dad never complained much about the treatments, you usually never knew of most of the side effects and how it was effecting him until you were sitting with him in the doctor office and hearing what he needed help with, some type of adjustment to maybe help with the discomfort or side effects. There was always that cycle of getting tired and weak, maybe some side effect of rashes, loss of appetite, pain, breathing problems to adjust to,worry about getting a temperature or a cold or increase in symptoms, then regaining some of the strength back then starting the cycle again. There were some moments of things getting better, but toward the end of the treatments, the cancer adjusted to the treatments and again took what it wanted and began taking the path it wanted. So when all of the treatments were done, the plan of action was changed from healing to making things as comfortable as possible for him. That transition from trying to get rid of the cancer to just having to allow it to take over, was a gradual one with steps. Coming to the conclusion you couldn't do anything to stop it and just it let it take it's path until whatever the end might bring wasn't an easy one. You now just didn't know what would come next, but knew it could be unpleasant. When Dad first heard the news the cancer was still growing, he knew it wasn't good, but he still was putting up a fight to make it the best he could. As he was told there was a feeling of silence and heaviness in the room. The nurses had left the chart on the table before the doctor had arrived to give the news, but me and Dad already knew it wasn't good. The chart was full of wordage that pointed to continued growth of the cancer and abnormalities of growth. You knew the road ahead would be getting harder with uncertainty what would come next. I knew he was trying to hold in the fear and what ever he was feeling at the time. I seen him talking on the cell phone coming home from the doctor visit in the car telling someone how the doctor appointment went, his eyes started to water up and a few tears came. His mouth started to quiver slightly before being able to regain his composure and continue on. I didn't really know what to say to him except to be there. After hearing the news the cancer was still growing it wasn't long until it would completely take over. At the time you didn't know how long it would take, what to do, where should he live, or what he would need. He had been living alone in his own place, soon he wouldn't be able to take care of himself anymore on many levels. The uncertainty of how long the cancer would take to finish it's path, the cost of medical expenses and the cost of where to live if needed. Would he incur large debt, just trying to live out his last few days or months. Dad's biggest fear was that of dying from suffocation. That feeling where you just can't get any air. You are panicked and you can't get that last grasp of needed air into your lungs but you keep grasping for it. That was the biggest fear for everyone, just not wanting that to happen, or just the fear of having him suffer like that causing his death. He went through a few episodes of struggling to fight for air toward the end before they were able to get things medically stable at the hospital. You could see that fear in his eyes when he was going through an episode. I remember him taking my hand on one of episodes in the middle of the night at the hospital to help himself somehow make it through it. I held his hand and rubbed his back hoping to give him some kind of comfort to relax and make it through until the medicine would kick in, or that is what you hoped for. It was hard to see him struggle through those episodes and you really couldn't do that much. They would start to occur when he had to do any kind of movement that exerted a lot of energy for himself, such as just getting to the bathroom or having to stand up and move a short distance. You could tell he was no longer much able to or should move from his bed. During the attacks you just wanted it to be over as fast as possible, to get that medicine in as fast as possible and wait, hoping it would kick in quickly.

Dad made it about one year after he was diagnosed with lung cancer. He had moved in with my brother and his family for a few weeks toward the end, where he was closer to the hospital to get more medical treatments. It did become apparent soon he needed to be in the hospital. He was having breathing attacks and was growing weaker. He was needing more medical care than could be given at a home setting. Being in a hospital is like being in a world of it's own. You encounter people who are struggling with their bodies and you have to take notice and take gratitude for having your own health, knowing that it can be taken from you at anytime or at some point in growing old. The setting is now between walls, a setting that seems to function as it's own away from the world that is happening outside. But being in the hospital and being able to leave are two different things. You also gain the gratitude of being able to walk out as you want, unlike having to be there with a sick body that holds you down. I was around when my grandparents passed away in a hospital setting but never really spent the time there, just short visits, so this was my first real experience of being there when death was knocking at the door, waiting for the door to be creaked open.

Dad's body was gradually shutting down, he longer had any appetite and was growing weaker. His bowels had shut down and you were just wandering what the next system would be and how it would effect his comfort. Dad seemed to keep that hope that things would get better for him physically, which at times was hard to hear. Part of it was just the confusion that was building, the regimen of meds knocking you out, being disoriented between days and nights and the uncertainty of when to fight and when to give into the death process. Knowing your going to die and actually facing that moment are two different things. It's always kind of hard picturing yourself in a state of might not existing anymore, and what that means for yourself and your life. Rethinking all of the steps and memories of a life lived. Dad said he was okay with how his life had been and was ready to go when it was time. Saying it is harder for you guys then on me, being there during those last moments. But he kept wanting to have tests ran to see if things could get working again or what could be done to get it fixed. We had always been in that mode and that is what we expected, to fix it. Now it couldn't be fixed. He did seem to

7

eventually accept the fact that things would not get better, but I think it was because he got too tired and weak and just needed to rest. When the battle was about over he was transferred from the hospital to a hospice house, since the hospital doctors concluded they couldn't do anymore and they could do the same thing in a nicer setting. I think we were all kind of surprised of how comforting the hospice house and the hospice workers were. Not that hospital staff are not good, but hospice is such a great program and support service without a large charge of expenses that take what you have left. They know about the death process and the transition we all will experience and provide some dignity and comfort in that process. Dad made it through one night at the hospice house. That last day and night he didn't seem to be in that much discomfort, just weak and tired. His alertness was minimal and his breathing at times would become loud, irregular and you could see the uncertainty from the faces of others who had been in his life now and as he was growing up. A life would soon be ending, but at the time we didn't know when. He was in the final stage of being here and his focus wasn't here in the physical as much but getting ready to transition to another place, at least that what was said in the hospice brochure literature on the process of how death occurs. He passed away in his sleep in peace during the night. I got woken up by the hospice nurse in the middle of night with a gentle tap on my shoulder while I was laying on the couch across from him in the room. I think I'll always remember the feel of that tap and quiet gentle voice of the nurse letting me know it was complete. I think it gave me a picture that there is some grace and peace at the end of a life even with physical struggles and fears of death. There was some sense of peace and respect intertwined with the nervousness of being at the end of a life. The scattered thoughts of being unsettled with the finality of it all. The hospice house was a place of peace and respect for families and loved ones, the way Dad and family wanted it to be. To show us it is okay to die with dignity and respect, even when the body is no longer able to function as we would want. I think it is important not only the way we live that counts but the way we die. The way we encounter those last moments. I know it was important to Dad, especially after experiencing the death of his son through taking his own life. Death on many accounts takes away many things, but it doesn't take it all.

My brothers ending of his life was a different kind of ending, one that I hope also will eventually end in peace and grace. Dad once said dying wasn't hard, but living could be hard. Now he was with Jason and others who have passed on. Life would continue, whether here or there or that is what I know Dad would wish.

My brother Jason died from suicide on October 22,1999. Jason was sixteen years old at the time of this death, the same age I was at the time he came into my world. Remembering the day he was born is intertwined with the sense of loss of the way his life ended. The moment of birth instilled in my mind and heart with the image of myself being in the high school gym shooting baskets with a school secretary coming in and telling me he had been born. I remember sitting down on the bleachers, but after that I don't remember much more about it, just those brief moments when I was first told, feeling proud and looking forward to having a little brother which is intermixed with the moment I heard he had passed.

Those brief sixteen years in between seem way too brief with only moments that I don't want to fade away with time and memory, only because it might feel too much like he never existed. At times it feels so much like a different time and a different world when he was here. I guess that is like any death, time moves on, people and situations come and go and life moves on. My daughter has some brief memories of Jason, but mostly just the pictures of him. It took me few years after his death to let her know how he had died. From time to time she would ask about him and his death, and I never got to the suicide. I guess I just wanted her to have good memories of him, somehow protecting her from that reality. I eventually ended up telling her when she was about eight or nine, when we went to the cemetery to drop off some balloons at his graveside to acknowledge a birthday gone by. She seemed to on some level to understand the sadness involved, looking into my eyes whenever she heard Jason's name. She knows Jason was my brother and her family and those brief memories that probably have faded now. As time passes it does seem like you lose a little part of them every year that passes. I miss those everyday conversations where you would be able to talk about him or what he was doing. They can't be seen, only felt and remembered in our hearts and inside of our souls. It's up to us to do that and how we do that. Now he is a faded memory, but still a strong influence of who I am and want to be. At times I've felt like I've learned from his loss, but have at times needed to take the time to stop and remember about those last moments of his life.

Suicide is a word that I don't think I'll ever get comfortable saying or talking about but it's word that I want to try to understand and feel what it is about. The journey for me has been about life, not death. It is about my journey, my brothers' journey and those along the way that are affected by suicide. It's about my healing and my hope of giving a voice for those who've lives seem to be ended short.

Really the first moment when I truly felt what it was like to feel what it was like to be experiencing the full array of emotions involved in the end of someone's life was sitting at the funeral home making arrangements for Jason's funeral. At other funerals I felt part of the feelings but could hold them a length away and not fully experience them altogether, With Jason's death I couldn't because they washed over me and was I forced to feel it. I made attempts to hold in the pain but it was too painful physically to do it. As I was sitting around with the family the first few days before the funeral, details about his death and that final day would slowly come to awareness and each new detail was like a new wave of pain that would come inside of me and couldn't be stopped, feeling like a piercing of a knife in the middle of my chest. If I made attempts not to cry, it would just hurt. I couldn't stop those waves of pain, only endure them. As time went by those waves decreased, but it's something that stays with me. Something I've never felt before that, and never want to forget the depth of those moments. Those moments of pain, brought pain but it also brought me to more understanding and compassion for those in pain.

I wasn't really wanting to be involved in making the decisions and the arrangements of the funeral, mostly just taking it in and observing and thinking this shouldn't of been happening. It just didn't seem natural for him to die so young and the way he did. Dad was going through his own issues of feeling guilty or a feeling he had let Jason down in some way. My Mom was probably more like me, a little more introverted and dealing with the issues on her own terms and away from the noise of the day. Anyway the details of the final days got taken care of and life slowly moved on. Those little details of how you wanted Jason's life to be represented of who he was were magnified. What to put in the obituary, what to have him wear, would he look like he did in life? Could you tell he had shot himself in the temple of the side of his head? Going through the room with a combination of different coffins, trying to pick out one that would somehow represent Jason. My Dad getting weak and going to one knee and getting help up looking at the coffins. My Mom looking at Jason one last time in the casket before the funeral whispering that he was just sleeping. Those strange brief moments that stand in time and memory. You never really think about all of those little details about a person that makes them unique and who they are or you take them for granted. Years after Jason's death there are times I still just want to watch and stare at my daughter who is growing so fast, trying to catch all of the little details about her and her life. Of course she does not like me staring at her and watching her and will let me know. She doesn't know the storyline about it. Some of that is just trying to take time to appreciate her and some of it is fear, with that feeling any day could be that last day. Knowing that she is growing and changing and wanting to hold unto her at that moment. The way they smile, the way they wear their hair, the clothes they wear on a regular basis. Seeing a piece of paper with their writing on it that is uniquely theirs. The things they like to do or have made that will stand in time and represent a stoppage of time for those who've passed on. Thinking of those missed future moments of a shortened life for Jason. It is said when you lose a parent you lose some of the past and when you lose a child you lose the future.

We picked out a Kenny Rogers song about a young boy being a baseball pitcher that fit a part of Jason's life in playing baseball for a funeral song. When you thought of Jason, you thought of baseball. I missed a lot of being around when he was growing up, but remember when he had first started playing baseball. At first he had backed out from signing up, anxious whether he could do it or not, then one year he did sign up and started pitching for the teams he played on. It's kind of all mixed up in my head the memories of those days. I just remember it was a joy to watch him play. He was one of the better pitchers on each team each year he played. He would get into situations where he needed just that one more out or strike, and more than often he would get it. He seemed to be able to handle the pressure and just do what was needed to get out of trouble and win the game. I know Jason never got to really feel the joy he brought to us watching him play baseball through the years. I suppose as a kid you don't understand that or feel it, but as I get to see my daughter play sports it brings me back to those days of being able to watch a child play sports and the enjoyment that brings, if only a break from the grind of daily work. So that Kenny Roger's song in a way was a tribute to the appreciation of not only who he was but those times watching him play and what that brought.

A friend of my Dad's was called to do the ceremony at the funeral and the pieces were coming together for the end of a life. Running to the store where Jason had been working to arrange for flowers for the funeral, going out to look for an ear ring to put in his ear since he had one in life. Recognizing that's what is important to do for him, but mostly for ourselves. Wanting the funeral and the ending of his life to represent who he was and what he had meant to us. Dealing with the questions and seeking answers of what had happened to want him to take his own life was a gradual process. Knowing that the answers may never come but wanting to know some of them. Part of me had some distant angry feelings toward the funeral director, thinking he does this kind of thing on a regular daily basis. Was this just another job for him and money gained from a death, at the same time feeling respect and admiration for the role he does. What would it be like to being dealing with death and families on a daily basis? Does death just become routine.

I wasn't really sure what I would feel seeing him laying in the coffin motionless and lifeless and expressionless. I still don't really know what I feel about it though I felt how the reality that physical life does end and will end and could happen at any age. After a few days going through the visitation and the actual funeral seeing him laying there, it did give some eerie comfort being able to see that physical connection to him. Toward the end it brought about the knowing that his body would be soon gone. He would be buried beneath the ground and time would move on. That process of trying to seek answers of what happened was intertwined with seeking closure with the funeral.

The day of his death had started out just like any other day. That's the thing with bad things happening on any given day. Things seem normal and then there's that sudden change you aren't expecting or would want to happen. That sudden change feeling that stays with you for awhile, maybe forever in some form your not even aware of. That being combined with the gained knowing that you should appreciate each and every day and the people in your life. Sometimes you don't show it, or the feeling they didn't know how you had felt about them. With suicide it's that sadness of seeing someone's life ending because they didn't or couldn't feel the goodness of themselves or life.

The last time I seen Jason was when he was at his after school job at the local Hy-Vee grocery store. He was sacking groceries and I was paying for my items in another lane about twenty feet away. Standing there watching him work briefly while in the line and thinking of how proud I was of him, with a little grin on my face. He seemed to be so grown up, having his first job, wearing a nice white shirt and tie on, and looking handsome. He had seen me but he quickly looked down and didn't make an acknowledgment of me at the time, appearing a little embarrassed about himself while I was there. He didn't feel those feelings of being proud of what he was doing or who he was.

The day of his death had started for me before I ever knew what was going on. I was at his work that early afternoon at Hy-vee in the parking lot getting ready to leave when I seen my Mom heading into the store. She seemed in a hurry and a little distraught but I didn't have time to catch her and didn't really think much of it. Later that night I would connect it together with the happenings of the last day. By the time the news hit me it was early evening. It's never good when a policeman comes to you asking you to call family. Not knowing what to expect, hearing the sense of loss in my father's voice as he told me. The answers you wanted to know that wouldn't come. Along came a sense of shock, with trying to catch up with what you have just heard.

After his death, I would catch myself at times in the same line and same place looking over to where Jason had been working where I had seen him last. It wasn't Jason there anymore, just some other person busy doing the job as if nothing had happened with short glimpses of memory of him being there and those feelings of the time before faded into the past. That sense of the last moments of someone's life carries over at times with other people. It's something that will happen again you just don't know when.

With suicide it is about seeking answers about that last day. About those last moments and thoughts and feelings. Those last moments don't have to define a person's life but they do more than any other kind of death. Being able to get past that defining moment has been a part of the healing process for me.

The first questions that arose were trying to find out what had happened that day. Why was it that day? What events had taken place to cause him to complete the suicide. That evening, and the following few days before the funeral the family gathered at my Mom's house questioning the events and themselves. We were trying to process the events of the day and previous days leading up to the suicide. That was the first time I heard of there was a previous attempt of him having suicidal feelings and actions. It kind of surprised me hearing that, a little angry that I wasn't told or knew of it. I don't know if it would of made of any difference or if I would of taken it different. Like any suicide it seems to happen so fast at the end. You think you have time. I had my own family at the time and wasn't around or involved since of the age difference and out of the house. I found out at that time Jason had a previous attempt of wanting to cut his wrist and not feeling life was worth living. I don't know really know a lot of details but an image inside of my head of what it might of looked and felt like. The events of the last day were pieced together as best as they could of over time after the funeral. When it came to piecing things together, it's hard to tell what is true and what is partially true. Things get a little off as the different stories come out. Rumors become different than facts, because they are lined with emotions and different perceptions. It became a drive by all of us, trying to piece those last few moments together, and what that would that would mean about his life. It was a school day and Jason made attempts to have someone take the day off with him, stopping by a girls house asking her to take the day off but she couldn't. He apparently might of tried with some other friends also to take the day off with him, but wasn't able to find anyone. It wasn't clear how far he made it to the school. Some stories came about that he made to the school but didn't make it in, other stories are that he had made it to the school that day but got in a argument with the vice-principal and got expelled and left. Whatever the story, Jason had started drinking alcohol and his inhibitions less intact. He had started out driving a car of my Moms but it got a flat tire. He had tried to change it but wasn't able to get the job done. He apparently had driven it for a while because there wasn't much of a tire left when he dropped it off at my Mom's house. He left the car after not getting the tire changed and got a spare car of my Dads. My moms car was left with images of the last moments that gave me eerie feelings looking at. The whole searching or trying to find physical clues to a death in itself is spooking and depressing. It's like looking at death itself. What I found in the car were some of the clues of the events of the day. I found his license on the floor, scattered with bullets and alcohol in the front seats of the car. I took his license and kept it for myself at the time. He had just briefly had gotten and I wanted something recent and something that nobody had. Something physical to be able to hold unto him a little longer. When we were looking for some kind of note to explain why he did. We found a piece of paper in the trunk with some ramblings of feeling like he couldn't do anything right and angry feelings. Most of it we couldn't be make any sense of. We ended up just throwing it away and kept it away from our parents. It wasn't really a suicide note but some clues of what he might of been feeling at some point. It was just a sad feeling combined with a loss of life ended in anger and sadness in the last moments, not how I wanted Jason remembered.

That last day was fueled with alcohol, anger and frustrations of the flat tire, feeling alone, and just wanting to end it all. Things just kept building up and it probably felt at that time life would always be like that. Jason had taken off in my Dad's spare car. He had gotten a gun and found bullets and was drinking and feeling like life wasn't worth living anymore. He was found several miles out in the country roads by a stranger, where he had shot himself. I've never really wanted to think about those last seconds of him pulling the trigger and what that must of felt like. Going to place of where it had ended with my Dad was a little eerie and sad, but I felt I had needed to see the spot. I don't really feel any need to go back there but maybe someday. I don't think anyone keeps it up, or even if it is there anymore since Dad has passed. It has one of those crosses in the ditch that you sometimes see along the highways where someone has passed. Those crosses along the highway reminds me of Jason and the sense of loss and grief it must bring to those who keep those crosses and flowers alive along the places of the barren ditches.

As we were trying to piece the events together, we had to try to find out how school had effected the last days of Jason's life. It was just part of the those questions that remained after Jason's death. There were rumors of him being expelled and not getting along with the school leaders. A few months before the event Jason and my parents were having some disagreements with the school. One day Jason didn't want to attend school because he had decorated his face for a school event showing school spirit for an homecoming event. It was raining that day and the make-up got messed up and he couldn't get it off. He was supposed to put some cream or something under it so it would come off easy. Well anyway he didn't want to go to school with his face paint all messed up and not being able to get it off. My parents didn't make him go and they called him in to take the day off. The school found out he wasn't sick so they counted it as skipping and gave him truancy with detentions to be attended. My parents had a meeting to discuss the situation with the principal to no avail. I remember my Dad saying he came out feeling small, which affected greatly the frustrations that would follow afterward. The school never did know why Jason didn't show up that day, they just knew he skipped and made the determination of the penalty over my parents decision of letting him take the day off. Jason during the time was feeling like what's the point and wasn't showing up for the detentions and the school hadn't let my parents know that. The day that Jason skipped school for the last time, the school didn't notify my parents at work as directed. They left a message at home stating Jason didn't show up. They got the message when they got home, way afterward the event had occurred. That was coupled with feeling or thought that maybe something could of been done to stop it. After the funeral we met with the school to sort out the rumors that had been floating around those final days. He hadn't been expelled or had contact with the principals that day, but my Dad still felt dissatisfied with the way the school had handled things over the previous months, and the feelings he had within himself that he had let Jason down in someway with the school situation. He went through the process of suing the school for not notifying them at work. It wasn't the main issue, just one of the issues that could be looked at legally. Eventually it was dropped but it was the process that my Dad wanted and needed to go through. I suppose that sometimes is the process of dealing with a death from suicide, looking for reasons or meaning.

Those days after the funeral were lined with those last days and moments of Jason's life. People who didn't know Jason had died, asking or calling for him. Letting a pen pal from a school project know about his death when a letter came for him. Those little transition details that come about that you have to deal with. Trying to sort it all out and how it came out and dealing with moving on and healing.

Sometimes when life becomes routine and I get in autopilot about the routine of life, it's good to think about some of these times to reflect on what the people in my life mean to me and the reality of having a last day for all of us, what that day may bring. Somehow the spirit and the memory of those who've passed help me understand that we don't have to be special, just ourselves, because that is what we miss the most and appreciate.

Talking to Someone

After Jason's death I knew I wanted to try to keep a connection with him, even it was considered unconventional. I wanted to know that I was still his brother and could be there for him and learn from him and his situation, even through he was no longer here. I knew I wanted to do it soon and knew on some level life had to be more than what we can see with physical eyes. I can't see a lot of things with my eyes or physical senses, does that mean it doesn't exist? So two weeks after his death I listened through a distant telephone call of someone who I had never met or known of before those moments. A person who is called a medium, those who say they can contact the energy of the "dead". It gave me an opportunity to talk to someone in detail about those last days and moments of Jason's life and Jason's life in general. That in itself was healing and I was grateful for the opportunity. I was able to talk about Jason and the way he had died and what he may of been feeling before he had died. It was like being able to be there with Jason, talking and listening to him just like he was in the room. Whether he was or not there didn't matter because somehow his energy was there, and it felt like it to me. That's something that couldn't be taken away from me whether you believed in it or not. The energy had an impact on me and my feelings regarding the situation and Jason. It was healing for me to be a part of it. My intention was to be his brother. I wanted to know if I could help him in some way and know if he would be okay. To understand, to be there in those moments, to heal and learn for myself. To me he was still my brother, I still wanted to feel a connection to him, and my version of what God is, wouldn't take that away from me or my brother.

I had nervous energy before making that first phone call. I paced back and forth waiting for the clock to tick down to the moment it was suppose to begin. I didn't really know what to expect and was hoping I wouldn't be disappointed in the process. Time finally came to the moment of making contact, and story would began. I went down to the basement trying to find a quiet place for privacy, but mainly just a place where my girlfriend at the time wouldn't know I was trying to contact my dead brother. I lived near railroad tracks at the time and trains kept coming through the area, and the reader could hear the train each time, which kind of relaxed the situation because it was kind of funny, getting interrupted by the sounds of whistle each time. It started out slow and uneven, to the point where the person felt there wasn't going to be a connection and was going to have to stop and try another time. That is when things started to speed up some. That's when it first made it real for me, it was just like Jason if he would of been there. He still had the personality, the feelings and emotions that Jason would of had. At first I knew he wouldn't of wanted to talk to me if he was "alive" Why wouldn't that be the case, wouldn't he have to start at where he was, just like I had to start out with at that moment in time. He still had feelings and emotions of being angry, frustrated and confused. He talked about some angry feelings toward my Dad, some feelings of how Mom had been trying to get into his space, or always commenting they didn't have money for this or that. He wasn't trying to blame anyone for his actions but thoughts in his mind were scattered and he had to place himself back into those last moments of time and try to put the pieces together and felt a need try to defend what had happened. It was described like trying to put together shattered glass. Things were fragmented in his mind still.

He still had some of his humor, commenting or asking me why I was hiding. The medium described my position in the basement in which I was more or less in a hiding position because I didn't want to be disturbed during the reading or found out I was trying to talk to the dead. It was put in a humorous way with my brothers' personality. I knew then my brother was okay but he was dealing with the emotions and had to deal with the thoughts of his physical death. He said it was just like school. He didn't like to go to school, he would rather be out playing, but had to be in a place like school or where he had to look at his life. He had work to do. He said your mad at me, but I felt like that all of my life. He wasn't really angry all of his life but those were the emotions that were running at the time from him. He had a hard time wanting to connect to me because as he phrased it, I don't want you to think of me as a loser. Those words hit me in the heart because that would of been what Jason would of said and I could feel that. It wasn't something I was thinking but I knew it would of been something Jason would of been thinking. Jason brought up how he had looked up to me as kind of a father figure. I was quite a bit older of him and he had looked up to me as an older brother or fatherly figure. That is something that I knew on some level but didn't really think about much or Jason and I didn't talk about until these moments. It was like being able to talk about issues that mattered even through he wasn't here anymore, at least in the physical. These are some of the moments that I would of liked of been able to talk to Jason. To connect more to him and know what Jason had been feeling and thinking. I had felt that connection but never was able to really discuss things with him. Those quick brief moments of talking on the phone with a stranger that never truly knew the impact of the words spoken. I asked the reader how I could let him know I hadn't or didn't think of him as a loser and she said you just did, he can hear and feel you. I could just feel his presence in the room within that moment and the impact of being able to say those words and a knowing that he had heard me is a feeling that stays with me. I wish in life I was able to have more of these talks with him. He mentioned he had always felt a good connection with me, where you just look at each and know what the other was thinking without having to talk, just that glance of the eyes or catching the humor in something alike that maybe others didn't get.

But I didn't get to be around him like same age siblings, I was sixteen years older than him and already out of the house when he was growing up. That was the other major theme that had came through. He had felt like he had been a mistake and should of never been born. My parents got divorced briefly after he was born. He came fifteen years after the last kid was born in the family. He gave an image of himself sitting on a couch with everyone else already moved out and he was left there alone. He had feelings of feeling different than the rest of his brothers and sister. Those thoughts during his life never really occurred to me or as far as I knew never got discussed. I never seen him as different or an outcast from the family. He didn't see his other brothers or sister go through the same things so he felt he was different or thinking we didn't have the struggles like he did. He mostly just seen us as adults. I didn't really know what was going on in his life because I was out of the house with my own family during the time. About the only time I got to talk to him was those brief times before or after a baseball game or those brief times I would see him around town walking with his friends.

We discussed things that he had liked or did bring him joy in life. Not everything could of been bad, could they? He brought up having the sense of pride of being an uncle. He stated he had felt a connection to kids and playing with them.

He felt a connection to his nephew and niece's, because they made him feel he didn't have to be anyone but himself. I mainly have images in my head of him laying on the floor with a group of nephews and nieces laying on him wrestling and playing around. He had enjoyed spending time with them when they were all around for the holidays or some get together. But he felt he would never have kids of his own, it just seemed to far away to touch. He was going through adolescence frustration trying to figure out what he wanted to do with his life. It seemed to overpower him or he over magnified his problems and it brought him way down. Baseball was asked about because that was something he was fairly good at, and recently had attended the state baseball tournament and had gotten a medal, something my Dad still had. He said baseball was an outlet but not something that could sustain him. He then brought up some regarding the computer he had just recently got, it was his first computer and was just starting to get to know how to use. After he died it went to a cousin because my Mom wasn't much into using computers. He brought up art, pointing out directions of where his art work was placed in my Moms house in which he did. After myself hearing that I started putting more of my daughter artwork she had done in school, getting them framed and put up like a regular picture like it was at my Moms house. It sort of gave me another connection to my brother and just the feeling of more appreciation for my daughter and her creativity. We then discussed some regarding his friends and buddies. He said he hanged out a lot. He talked briefly about the things he had did, going to the mall and hanging out, but felt bored a lot like he was waiting around for something to happen. He stated he hanged around with them but didn't really talk about things. He talked about girl he had liked and was still watching over. He talked about not liking the way he had looked. He had always been a little heavy, but recently had lost weight and had the girls starting to like him. I remember a co-workers daughter one day talking about him and being attracted to him. He did seem to have many friends, younger than him, older than him, boys and girls alike. So it was not a matter of not being liked. During the holidays one of his former friends stopped by Mom's house and brought their new baby to the house, they named the baby, Jason after him. His friends still stop by my parents house from time to time to visit. My Dad was like a second Dad to some of his friends. Jason brought up people and things he had done, that I wasn't aware of. That was exactly the way it was. Something I didn't really think about before the discussion but after his death during the phone call.

He had overtime gained a I don't care reckless attitude on the outside, but on the inside he felt too much. The reading kind of ended in a solemn way, he was okay, he stated he wasn't being judged or his death looked at as a sin, but he had to deal with his decision and try to heal from it. Briefly it was brought up that something physically was wrong with him that contributed to his choice, but it didn't get revealed until later sessions asking about it. Interesting parts of readings were that when doing them with the same reader, the reader I worked with at first didn't retain most of the reading the next time, so at least at first it was kind of like starting over and she would start to remember some of the feelings and images. I worked with three different main readers. With all of them it didn't take long to pick out how he had died. I didn't give any clues or discuss how he died, but they brought it up without clues. There was a continual of the story even with different readers, same exact statements were made at times. One reading talked about a baby in the family being born in the future, and I discussed or said I hoped it wasn't mine laughing. In another reading with another reader that topic came up and those exact words with the humor came up without myself saying anything, it was just a point of reference so there would be some knowing of connection. There was just a connection of being able to describe different physical settings such as houses and arrangements even through Jason hadn't been there in life in some settings. There were connection of events or happenings in my current life that were described, a planting of a tree in his memory. My Mom going to garage sales and getting me a chair and commenting how it was falling apart, putting humor in it saying what a bargain. Going to garage sales is a thing with my Mom so it would be something to comment on that is significant. Just events that I only would connect to or think significant.

They may not mean anything to someone else but they do to you. The readings were filled with that for me, those little details that connected me to a knowing that there has to be some energy or connection that this person is able to pick up without myself saying anything. Within grief, you can't really appreciate those little moments of connection. The physical connection of a body is gone so connections are blocked or not felt. The connection is more of a subtle energy.

As time passed and the readings continued, Jason became less defensive and seemed to enjoy the time as much as I was. He over time became less hard on himself. Part of his healing process was to regain that feeling of connection to others. In life he had only his perception of himself, now he was able to see and feel what others had felt and thought. He was able to see himself through different perceptions. Part of his time was spending time being around those he had been known in life, friends and family and again feeling connected to them and life. He discussed part of that physical problem discussed earlier was having an imbalance like having ADHD. It wasn't just about him being selfish or immature, he was having a physical problem that contributed that was making him more compulsive and angry, not sleeping, just not being able to slow down his thoughts and step back and see what was happening. He had been feeling depressed for awhile, but even toward the end he didn't think it was as bad as it was. He talked about alcohol contributing at the end, just lessening the inhibitions, alcohol giving him less control and acting more on it. Something he probably wouldn't of done with alcohol even through it had been on the back burner. He discussed some family past history of just not talking about things that was passed from generation to generation. The thought or feeling you should just be quiet and move on. That was geared mainly toward my Mom's side and dealing with an alcoholic parent. He was an alcoholic that got angry when he drank and eventually died from alcoholism. I never really seen him drunk, but remember others talking about how he shouldn't be drinking but he had continued drink until his death.

I later discussed some of these issues with my Mom. Jason wasn't diagnosed with ADHD growing up but after looking up the signs and going over them, it seemed pretty likely he had some form of it, showing a lot of signs and behaviors of it. My Mom talked to a cousin that has it, and he talked to her about some of his experiences in dealing with it. He had a doctor appointment the day he died. I don't know if they would of diagnosed it or not, but it never happened. She was also able to confirm feelings and the way it was like growing up with an alcoholic parent.

During one of the readings he stated I still had some anger toward him in the way he died, not being able to stick it out and live. I didn't really think I did at the time but probably did to some extend. He told me to go to the place where I liked to go, the place I go to get away to relax and think, to go there and he would be there. He described the place, a wooded area along the park paths. That was the place where I liked to walk and think at the time. I knew instantly where to go. He wanted me to work out the anger and to know he would there. I went there after a few days and took the walk and just accepted his presence there with me and thought about anger and way he had died. A short time later it did help me. I had been working with this individual who was always feeling suicidal. Everybody was just getting tired of it and didn't really know what to do. She had a long history of that, mostly it just appeared because of wanting attention. She hasn't ever acted on it, mainly just appearing to want attention or others to feel sorry for her. Not making active attempts, just wanting life to end for themselves. Hoping they would go to sleep and die. People were just getting angry with her and wanting her to stop. That's when I remembered having to deal with anger with my brother. I realized I couldn't judge whether this person had the right to feel suicidal or not. She was having those feelings and I needed just stop judging what she should be feeling and listen to where she was and why. Putting myself in her place, coming from a non judgmental place.

I think with anyone you need to listened to them in that state, not judging whether they have the right to feel that way or not. There are times on my job working with individuals who are depressed, who feel suicidal, where I come back to that anger and judgment. Just being able to listen to them and trying to understand where they are coming from without judgment intertwined with the knowing of the pain a suicide causes to others.

The last reading wasn't as much about Jason, but other family members coming through, some I haven't really thought about over the years, such as a cousin's husband, I didn't really get to know him but he was there in that circle of family that seemed to surround Jason during the readings. An uncle came through that was significant for me. It was a good feeling he was surrounded by family and the feeling was he would be okay. The other main person that I had wanted to connect to was my grandfather Cliff. He was able to come through the readings at times also, mainly just talking about taking Jason fishing. That was a significant remark because that was the strongest image I have of him. I spent a lot of my time with him fishing on the river, and have many fond memories of those times. I don't think Jason ever met him in life, passing over before he had been born. Just knowing Grandpa was there made me feel good. I always liked his energy and personality. As kids he would get sat down in his recliner and he would give us money for combing his hair while he fell asleep. I still have images of that small black comb and his thin gray hair that didn't really need combed, but it was something we always did and looked forward in doing so we could run to the store. We would take the money and run down to the old country store and get whatever, usually candy or baseball cards. Going to the store seemed so more exciting as a kid. You were able to pick out anything you wanted, of course with a limited amount, but as kid it is exciting.

He continued to "feel" lighter and was planning on helping other kids on that side and eventually stating he had plans to help kids on this side. Just being able to do the readings and be a part of his healing process, as well as my healing was comforting and rewarding. Even through I couldn't see him I continued to feel a connection that was beneficial to what seemed to both parties, living and the dead. Jason commented or used humor to say now he was now my bigger brother. I asked him what he would want to say to my parents if he could, he said to my Dad he wanted to be able to talk to him, to say he had his own life, his own choices. It wasn't about him, not what he did or didn't do. To my Mom he said he wanted to put his arm around her and give her a warm feeling of love, didn't want her to be attached to objects or the past that related to him. He was here in the present with her. He wanted others to know he was okay and he was sorry.

I think you do get to see a little more of the bigger picture of life when we pass. At the end it was stated it was just his time. He came here for what he needed and left. He had experienced what he had wanted. I don't know if it could of been different or not, I probably never got to see an even bigger picture of it all. It was a good feeling although knowing he was not only doing well but being able to help others. This is the story that had unfolded in front of me over the telephone, whether it was guided by a stranger or just my own thoughts or desires it had became healing. I never have done another reading in regards to connecting to him since those first two years of his death, about seven years ago. For some talking to the dead is not healing or just strange. Death is a closed veil of endings. One dilemma had been was how to reach out to the people who he couldn't. The better solution would of been to work out these issues while he was alive. I guess you could say the healing journey is of a personal nature, what one person needs or wants another person doesn't need or want. Some people are in a place where they need a definite line between the living and the dead, and with some maybe the line isn't so defined. Things work out as they need to.

Working Out the Issues

Suicide is a kind of solution that can leave others confused, angry, grieving and never giving a chance to see what life could of been. It also creates a boundary between the answers and the questions bounded by the boundaries of life and death. It's really more than finding answers it's having that lack of being able to work out issues or feelings with the people involved. It can leave everything in a holding pattern, where things remain the way they ended or just retaining memories of what was or could of been. This is the area that probably has had the biggest impact on me, especially as a parent myself. That possibility or knowing that someone young has died, it somehow just seems unnatural to how things should work. I find myself dealing with my own inadequacies on raising my daughter trying to separate my issues from my daughter issues she has to go through. At times I feel myself connected to memories of Jason in pain ending his life and seeing my daughter in pain, whether it's from anger, frustrations or just the steps of growing into adulthood. Not wanting those memories of ending a life in sorrow and frustration to repeat itself. Even though that may be the extreme result it is part of reality of life after seeing it happen. So part of working out the issues is for the survivors of being impacted by it.

The other aspect is the feeling of frustration of not being able to make the bridge between the living and the "dead" for others. Working out the issues with the person who has committed suicide is voided. Those times during the telephone readings, there were times where words, images in my head and heart connected just like he was in the room. Whether it was just in my imagination or wanting to hear what I wanted to hear, it doesn't really matter, because it was just as much reality to me as if he would of been there physically. It had an impact on me whether he was there or not. Those connections that were made were exactly what I needed to hear or feel, because they at times were connections only Jason and I had. Those personal connections that I couldn't totally connect to be real for another person or feel the impact that it had on me. Part of my healing process was in a form of prayer I suppose. I spent some time just thinking about the good feelings I had about Jason. Those times I had spent with him and enjoyed his company. I thought of the day we went to my Grandma's house and helped her dig up potatoes in her garden and putting them in storage. Jason wasn't very big at the time, but he wanted to come and help and be with me as I did him. It was a hot, dry summer day doing something that wasn't much fun, even so, we enjoyed being together and he liked being around his big brother. I got a chance to be with my little brother who looked up to me and I didn't have to compete with, at least from my angle as a big brother. I just thought of those moments we had spent together and what I would of wanted him to know if I would of had the chance. That was the basic feeling I had toward him. It was somewhat fascinating and enjoyable to be able to see him grow up intertwined with some feelings of loss of not being able to be around or connected to him as I would of liked because of the age difference and not being around. I wasn't really aware of the turmoil that was going on the inside of him and his life until after his death. It was as if he had received those feelings and emotions and was able to see himself through my eyes. That is something that in life sometimes we don't get to really know or feel because words can't quite describe it as you would want to or not just having the opportunity to have those moments. There were many moments in the readings that just hit right on with with times when you weren't quite sure where it was going, often leading to something but not always. I didn't always hear what I wanted but what I needed at the time. Having events discussed with the feelings and a knowing Jason knew what was going on in our lives, not just the external happenings but internal feelings and emotions. If it wasn't Jason it was some energy or way of being where things were connected together where we are not alone in the universe in our trials and tribulations. You couldn't hide behind a shield or face in this world of thoughts. I think that is a part of heaven or the other side. You are more aware and conscious of how others feel and why things happen and act. There isn't as much of judgment and putting people in labels and judging people as less or more. I did readings two weeks after Jason's death, and then about two months and six months, with a follow up in about two years. I did it over a time period because I wanted to see the progression of things over time, which I was able to experience. I also did it with other people in order to see if there were connections and there were. The stories connected and the story continued not dependent who I was talking to during the readings. I was able to work through some of my issues and at the same time felt I was able to help Jason work through some of his issues. I was able to feel like that was validated during the process. Knowing my thoughts, prayers and actions did have an impact on the "invisible". You probably can't really get the experience unless your open to it.

A common experience with individuals with who have suicidal tendencies can be a sense of invisibility. A sense of not being heard or seen, or not worthy of being seen or heard or alive. It's a perspective where you feel others don't understand you, or maybe you just understand yourself. A feeling like your going through something alone, a sense of isolation. A thought or perspective of others not going through it before and not feeling validated for your thoughts and emotions and feelings. There may be an impulse toward doing something to make an impact on others, whether it's some kind of acting out behavior or suicidal gestures to gain some kind of acknowledgment of validation.

Those connections of doing the readings is something I wish I could of given to others, especially those close to him but I wasn't able to. Talking to the dead may at first seem unnatural until you actually do it. The past is just a part of who we are now and who we become. It's a personal choice based on beliefs and what the person wants and needs for themselves. The readings always came to back to trying to connect to the living in some way, especially my Mom. There was no special messages in the readings except what being alive is about. Jason didn't become void of feelings or emotions. He didn't lose that sense of connection to others or become instantly wise and happy. He continued on his journey of healing and was trying to piece it all together just as we were. As time has passed, all of issues didn't or couldn't be worked out but life was moving on and the reality that each of us is responsible for our life's prevailed, whether here or there. Forgiveness, understanding and peace can also prevail, along the intersections of life. The messages were always try to connect to others, letting them know he was okay, he was sorry, and wanting to be there for them in their sorrow. That was in turn a frustrating part of connecting to the afterlife images and communications regarding Jason. I suppose there has been more awareness or acceptance of the concept, or it has became more entertaining then just scary and weird. From my world it is fairly acceptable to feel or think that there is something more beyond this world but not use of mediums. The connection is more one way, us connecting with them in our own way with faith through God.

Overall I think the hope and dream in regard to connecting to the Dead is to be able to have the opportunity to be reunited when it is time. To give Jason a big hug and see his smile again. I was able to discuss some of those big issues that did feel good talking about. The issues were real issues that I would of wanted to talk about the Jason's life and death. The other part of the story was trying to portray that life continues. I wanted somehow have others be able to work out some of their issues or their grieving in the here and now and not have to wait until they have passed also. To have a connection to the "dead" you can better recognize what are the things that are important or how others are important to you.

There are different paths to healing after someone dies, sometimes the path is not a straight path or a your path may not be healing to another person. Part of what I used for my healing process was my belief and hope that life wouldn't end at physical death. We remain with the personal connection that is felt but not seen. It revolves around those private thoughts and feelings of connection. After Jason's death I wanted to delve into that separation that death brings upon us. This is a story of what might happen if life didn't end at the moment of death. This is a story of a life ending in suicide and it's after affects if life didn't end.

With suicide the wish is that you won't have to deal with any feelings or emotions. To a suicidal individual, to be unconscious means to be in a state of tranquil quiet, a nothingness, an oblivion that is total and complete. Problems are not merely taken care of, there are no problems. There is no consciousness or the possibility of problems or anything else. The goal is cessation of consciousness. Your in the state of just being tired of feeling anything. You don't have the energy or the desire to feel or experience anything anymore. I think Jason did have those moments after death. A moment of surrender of life, a moment of feeling of relief of not having to feel anything, but it would soon pass back into the reality of what had happened. I don't think we can escape ourselves, whether we are here or there. We can escape for short periods but can't escape with what is. It's not about sin or judgment from God, it's just about life and living. We have to forgive ourselves before healing can take place. Most people judge themselves harsher than any God. You can tell that from the Bible. During the time of the Bible writings the people of that time needed God to be stern and harsh. Everything was about sin and being killed for various acts against God. As time has passed people have needed God to be less harsh and more about love. You have to look at what has changed, God or people views over what is. One of the overall concept of any religion is the belief that there is life after physical death. What gets you there and what that entails is for God to decide in most faith based religions. Life is portrayed as waiting for judgment. The point where an individual regains consciousness isn't quite clear, just after some point of judgment. On the other spectrum there can be the belief just having one life and everything is ended.

If Jason still had consciousness or life he would know what had happened. He would be able to describe what he had been feeling and thinking at the time and currently. Consciousness wouldn't of been ceased to exist. He might even be more conscious than before, because he could be able to see the effects of his actions. He would be able to sense the grief he had caused by his actions. This of course would be based on the concept that memory still exists. If there was just a clean slate where nothing from the "past" existed for you and you lived in heaven or hell as described in the Bible. But in that case you wouldn't know or remember why you were in "heaven" or "Hell". Life would be just a series of unconnected moments. Would Jason feel a connection to his past? Would he feel a connection to the people he had in his life or would that be muted in a state of slumber sleep for a later time of resurrection and judging. Think of those individuals waiting thousands of years or more to be resurrected. What would there life be like with the different time periods? This is a story about Jason having life, in a different form of the physical perhaps. We don't think of God just in physical form, so couldn't part of who we are be beyond physical form. Beliefs are just that, they are what you think could be or what reality is for you. Death is related to religion and God. There are many different religions and beliefs but they all seem to fit the individual and where they are and who they are. Basically on some level they have the same ideas and hopes, just at different levels or angles. That concept that there is something bigger than the individual ego that guides life. The concept that there is a journey of the soul. The soul part of us that survives physically death, and is able to transcend into more learning and growing. That souls are at different stages of growth and perspectives of what life is and what life is about.

The common action of suicide is to escape. Sometimes you can't always escape your pain. You have to work through it, to look at it, to try to understand it, go through it, instead of around it. That was what life was about for Jason after his physical death. He had to work on understanding himself and heal, just like we do, the living. What would be the purpose of it all if it wasn't that way? Anguish itself doesn't cause suicide, but the concept of lethality does. The idea that you can stop the pain if you kill yourself and stop the ongoing activities of life. The moment that the possibility of stopping consciousness occurs to the anguished mind as the answer or the way out, then the igniting spark has been added and the active suicidal scenario has begun.

The common purpose of suicide is to seek a solution. Suicide is not a random act. It is a way out of a bind, a difficulty, a crisis, an unbearable situation. For Jason, it would be to cease consciousness, to not have to deal with a sense of failure or not succeeding in life or not getting the things he had wanted in life. Not to have to worry about his future or feelings of anger and frustration. He had felt there wouldn't be anything that would of made things better. Everything ends in death anyway, so why go on and try. Life is a dead end. It did erase opportunities and choices. With depression and suicidal tendencies a person may feel there are no choices or options available. Their thoughts are constricted to the narrow choice of death as their only opportunity.

He was able to remove himself from his set of circumstances. He wasn't able to change what had happened. It was a permanent solution to temporary problems. He had a different set of problems and dilemmas to conquer and now he knew he couldn't just erase them with a single action. Imagine what it would be like to awake, still conscious after making such a drastic move and realize it didn't solve anything but create more painful feelings for yourself and others. He recognized he would have to work through those feelings and emotions that had drove him to the choice of suicide. Jason wouldn't be given instant wisdom, but had to go through the process of understanding why it happened, seeing the results of his actions. What other process would there be? Would you just magically be happy and wise? It's not a place of judgment or punishment or a place of being stuck. Is it a place of life or void.

Hindsight with Suicide

One of my first personal experiences of suicide I have is with a kid in my small hometown that I grew up with named Rick. I knew him from first grade to the high school years, which is when he passed from suicide. I still remember those early days of knowing him in early grade school. Remembering those feelings on how I had felt when I was around him. Most of the times I may not really remember people's names from the past, but I can remember how they made me feel, whether that brings about positive or negative feelings. I still remember Rick and some of those moments of knowing him. He seemed to be a kid that didn't quite fit in or that is what seemed to me. As a young kid in the early grades I just remember feeling a little uneasy being around him. He seemed to have a little chip on his shoulder, pushing others away, trying to show an image of being tough or being angry with the world in some way. He demonstrated to me an attitude of I don't care but probably cared more than he would show. He would eventually just give up trying to fit in, which he did by leaving the world. Rick was a coach's kid and because of that I think he had wanted to do better in sports or at least was expected or hoped for. His Dad was the coach on the team where Rick and myself played on the team. He was a kid who didn't have a lot of athletic ability and was overall small in stature. He didn't get to play a lot during the games, even with his Dad being the coach. I'm not really sure how that affected him, but I remember him trying out for another team and not making the team, which ended his baseball career. I'm not really sure if he had wanted to try out for the team or it was expected of him. He did seem to be always in some kind of fighting mood trying to proof something he couldn't. I still remember lining up against him playing football in P.E. class. He was gritting his teeth, saying how he was going to knock me down. I just kind of ignored it and him and avoided him altogether. That is probably what I remember most of him, trying to avoid him or not pay attention to him.

The last time I seen him was when he came over to my house on a warm, sunny day during the summer that year. It was the first and only time he had came over and knocked on the door. I was caught a little off guard, seeing him standing in the house wanting something or something to do. I think he came over to see if we were playing baseball that day or maybe he just felt a need to connect to someone that day. I would never know for sure. I don't really remember what he wanted but I remember him not staying long. He had a whole different energy to him. He wasn't that kid who was angry or a chip on his shoulder, he somehow seemed unsure of himself and was nice. It kind of caught me by surprise and at the time I didn't know what to think of it, because it was so brief and different from what I was used to.

The other strong image of him toward the end of his life was at the beginning of a school day. We were at the lockers getting ready for classes, kids were coming and going in the hallways and lockers as in any other day. I remember looking over and seeing Rick in the middle of two kids teasing him and him feeling flustered. They had his cowboy hat and were playing keep away with it and laughing about the fun they were having. He was trying to get it back and they were somewhat making fun of him and the situation. He had that drop of energy of why is this happening to me. I don't want to have to deal with this anymore. I at that point remembering thinking to myself of the possibility he might try to end his life. It was only a split second of my thinking it, but remember having the thought cross my mind. He just had the energy of being tired and feeling like things wouldn't change for himself. After that point he had started a don't care attitude and was just more reckless about things in some way. With hindsight looking back things seem a little more clearer but at the time they are somehow there but not totally conscious to do something about. Looking back at it, I don't know if I could of did anything but I didn't really try. It seemed to happen so fast toward the end. You never really expect it but you can see the signs more clearly looking back at it. That is one of difficult aspects with suicide, there are usually signs and actions there and you are left with the what ifs. If I or someone would of done this or that differently or even if I or someone would of did just a little more. After his suicide I sat in the high school lounge listening to the kids who that day had been teasing him and talking about how stupid it was that he had killed himself and still making fun of him for doing such a thing, trying to figure out why he did it, stating they hadn't dislike him. Part of me was angry toward the other kids because they weren't able to see how he had been feeling and part of me was sad, because I on some level had knew how he had been feeling and didn't do anything about it, just observing it play out. But even through I did on some level understand him and what he might of been feeling, I didn't really expect he would of killed himself, but it wasn't a surprise when I heard it. I didn't really think much of his suicide until after Jason had died, because they both had passed about the same age. I had to think about why I had felt disconnected to the situation or didn't try to reach out to Rick, knowing he had that energy of just being tired and not wanting to deal with things and his destiny in the physical. Part of it was just his personality. I didn't ever really feel comfortable or connected to him. He seemed to be in his own battle with himself even as a grade school kid when I first had met him. The other issue was just not wanting to be teased like he was, because of my own issues of going through it all earlier in the middle school years. Going through and making it through those teenage years does help me give insight on just how hard it can be. Kids can be cruel and thoughtless and your just trying to become who you are. I had been one of the those teenagers who had hit puberty before the other males in my grade. There were many physical changes and I hadn't been prepared for. I developed acne on my face, my hygiene appeared to change. I developed more body odor than before because of the changes. One day as adult with my daughter watching me getting ready for the day, she asked me why was putting Noxzema on my face. It came from those days of having acne and feeling ugly and out of place. Having those experiences at the time made me feel isolated and alone. Twenty five years later going by that school and area of those days,it brought me back to some of those emotions. Feeling the ghost of that young 12 year old boy walking around the ground area during recesses just trying to find a place to hind in a large group of scattered kids. The school, long ago had shut down, new houses were built on the playground we used to play on, but the spirit of those days was still there inside of me.

During those two years of going through the teasing and humiliation, I did learn some good things about myself. I kept most of it all inside me although and didn't tell anyone, but it comes out anyway. The anger, the lack of confidence, feeling worthless had to go somewhere and be dealt with. At the beginning it had started coming out on my younger brother, who was a year younger than myself. It didn't take much for him to make me angry and I would take it out on him by hitting him. Well that couldn't last long because my parents were there and I had to deal with the consequences of hitting him. Plus I knew I wasn't really angry at my brother. He was just the one there who I could express those feelings of wanting to release anger on something. That's when I found running. I found running helped me get out of that tension and frustrations of the day. I continued that feeling of just wanting to hide in the shadows. I ran near our house behind a wooden area, going back and forth about 40 yards, because that was the length of the woods that could hide me. Eventually I started to run around the yard area around the house. It took me awhile before I actually got out in the street and roads because that feeling of not wanting to be noticed so I could be left alone. Running probably was one of most powerful thing that helped me make it through those times. I could release tensions and frustrations and had some peace while I was doing it. It increased some my self confidence because at least in my small school I was one of the better runners and got some accomplishments from it. I never did quite as well as I could of doing those track and cross country events because those feelings of feeling worthless from those past experiences. Running in competition, it felt like at times I was wearing a fifty pound monkey on my back. I was trying to prove my worth, and looked at it how I did as how worthy I was. There were times when I just ran by myself or when I didn't feel like I had to prove anything. It was like floating. I felt like I could run forever. By the time I had gotten to high school, the teasing had stopped. The way those kids, who had teased me for their own pleasure made me realize I never wanted to be like that. It had given me a sense of what it was like to feel those moments of Rick being teased for the way he looked and who he was. I didn't tease Rick but I also didn't stand up for him. I suppose because I wasn't strong enough at the time. As an adult you can put it in the context of kids just being kids. Kids are cruel to each other, some kids really can't put themselves in perspective of how they make others feel especially at young ages. I suppose they too are just trying to fit in also. Time and events move on. We all probably have some memories of childhood that are ugly or are perceived by us during the childhood years. Suicide wasn't a choice for me, I somehow had the energy to deal with wanting to live, but I do remember that energy of Rick of not having the energy of dealing with it anymore or the resources to deal with it.

Working in the Mental
Health System

I've realized over time, I don't always connect things together in a conscious way at times. It does seem helpful to write down my thoughts, experiences and perceptions of events of life to see where they lead. I first wanted to start writing about my experiences to somehow get others to believe there was something real after death. What ever part that remains after death, part of it has a connection to the humaneness that is inside all of us that is intertwined with the spiritual. I wasn't able to convey that connection I had wanted to portray, so it went into just writing and it became more of a healing process I've done for myself.

I didn't revisit the concept of suicide until later doing a job in the mental health field working with mentally ill individuals in a care facility and later in the community. From time to time you do encounter attempts and completions of suicide. Attempts are more common than completions, which probably is good at least. One individual I knew made the attempt by cutting his throat. He cut his throat area then came out to the aide station bleeding. He would be okay beside the stitches and scars from the cutting. I remember after getting medical care he seemed somewhat embarrassed by having the scars to remind him of that day. There have been other individuals that I've have known who had completed the suicide, but hadn't seen them for awhile before hearing about it. It is gives you a sad feeling that someone feels a need to end a life in that way. One person had hanged themselves in their apt., and the other I'm not sure how they had passed, but hearing it was suicide. You don't really know what to think or do after hearing someone die unexpectedly like that, just that sense of loss of life ending in pain.

April fools day is one of those days that stand out for myself, not just for the yearly tradition of it being April fools but it being intertwined with hearing of the death and suicide of an individual I had been working with. One of the difficult decisions with working or knowing an individual who is depressed is when to hospitalize a person or just when to seek professional help. When it is voluntary it is easier, but if it is not, where the person has to be committed whether to a hospital, some kind of facility, or just getting them to see a doctor, it can be more of a difficult situation. The court has to be involved and the rights of the individual are involved. Sometimes people are sent to the hospital not because it will be helpful, but the belief it will be safer. We tend to think the problem is solved by getting the person in the hospital. While hospitalization may be the only answer to a severe suicidal crisis, it can be expensive, frequently crippling and stultifying. Very often hospitals devote their efforts to monitor the patients, preventing and controlling to keep the person safe but not therapy. They are not usually kept very long for effective treatment and follow up is not usually there. But sometimes it can give a person a break, and that's all they need. True suicidal prevention might address the problem before people reach the point of crisis, before they call the hotline or appear in the emergency room.

You can have foresight with suicide, where you do see the signs and behaviors that lead to attempts or a completed suicide. Individuals who have suicidal tendencies often will have times that will come and go with those intense feelings. When things are going well, you think things will be okay and possibly over with the tendency. But as bad times or events come up and they usually will, you might see the signs and behaviors creep up again. You don't want to overreact, but you have the concept of hindsight in the back of your mind. With suicide you can usually always look back at the history and previous events to see how it all led up to the final event. It just becomes more apparent and your left sometimes with thinking of what could of been done differently. You do what you can to help and support, but it doesn't guarantee the person will or will not act on those past suicidal tendencies, especially if there is a substantial history of suicidal tendencies. Hindsight is what you have with suicide. The clues are usually there, the past history is there in some way. That's the difficult part sometimes afterward. Not all people who emit clues commit suicide, but most people who commit suicide have the signs consistent with suicide. Human nature and instincts are set up to protect itself, so when that doesn't happen it can come as an unexpected shock. Nobody can control or be with someone all of the time, if they want to do something they will eventually do it. Even if you know the signs and know how to intervene, it doesn't guarantee suicide won't occur, but it can help. Even through knowledge and awareness can help, sometimes the clues that are there don't quite register when they are happening or your not sure what to think of them, or not thinking there bad enough to want a person to kill themselves. It can be very stressful for family and friends to be involved with a consistent suicidal individual, because you have the reality of knowing it could happen at some point, but not knowing for sure or when, will it be the next time. I've read statements of people stating there was some relief when it did happen, because at least now the worry was over.

Overtime working with individuals who have a mental illness, I've encountered at different times those who've become suicidal. Mental illness can decrease coping skills and just the stigma of it can lower self-esteem. Mental illness is chemical or genetic in nature, it's not always about how hard the person is trying or not perceived as trying. Stress does have an impact on the illness, just like any illness physical in nature. A lot of times the therapy is meds and interventions of counseling and supports with developing skills to better cope with stress.

One of my first direct encounters working on the job with a completed suicide was hearing that phone message on the answering machine that April Fool's day. I looked at my caller ID and I knew it was a call from work, so my first inclination was just to let it ring and take the message and call back if I needed to. It wasn't time for me to go to work yet, so I didn't really want to answer it. In some ways I guess I was glad I didn't take it. It gave me sometime to react or get away by myself before having to deal with the reality of it all. Hearing that message that John had killed himself made me replay those events of knowing him and those last moments with him. The events of knowing him had come to ending that day.

It all had started out before I really ever had talked to him. One summer, when I was a kid I went on vacation with my parents to Florida where his parents lived. His father was a friend of my Dad's. We went down there to see them and the sites and sounds of Florida. I just briefly remember him, we had spent the time mostly with his Dad, with his Dad taking us out for a meal and taking us see the sites. I remember feeling grateful to him for spending time with us. I just remember John as a young kid out playing with not a worry to his mind. Years later I would meet him again when he moved into the place where I was providing support services. He was now a young man, no longer that boy who I had briefly ran into on that family vacation. He had previously played in a band, having long hair and that image of a guitar in his hands. He got a job at a tire place shortly after moving into the apartment site. It was a large apartment building, not the best of shape because of the age and condition, but it was a place to live. A few years later it got torn down and replaced. For me it was a little strange him being there, he didn't know me until I told him about that time my family came to visit in Florida. I don't really know how much he had remembered of those times, but it was a small connection I had with him in some way. Getting to know someone in a mental health setting is different than just a casual day to day setting and environment. You not only have to get to know them you have to know why they are there, issues they have and private issues in what seems such a short amount of time. Your asking questions you would not normally ask a complete stranger, that takes time to build that trust and understanding of each other. Sometimes I think there is that feeling of boundary of they on that side, trying to deal with their problems, those needing support, and us, the mental health provider with the answers and authority. We all have our own issues and struggles, but the focus is on them and their issues and struggles, which is where in most cases is where the focus needs to be. I had that brief connection of him and his family and knowing him. I always feel a little awkward in first getting to know someone, and that was the same with John. I was just starting to get to know him, and then there was the end. The weekend before he had killed himself there was a group activity of a camp out. He had attended the campout and had spent the weekend with us. He had seemed okay but somewhat quiet. Soon after arriving home from the camp he had called me on the emergency pager with the feelings of feeling suicidal. I remember feeling tired from the campout, but soon went over to his apartment to talk to him about what he had been feeling. At the time I was concerned with the way he had been feeling but wasn't sure what to do about it. He felt he would be okay in his apartment and didn't want to go back to a mental health institute or hospital of where he had came, so I called my supervisor to get some advice, and he suggested having him sign a contract stating he wouldn't harm himself. I continued talking to him and wanted him to call me if he was still feeling suicidal, which later that night he did call me to let me know how he was doing. I made the judgment he would be okay. At the time I didn't want to make the situation worse by having him committed or making him go somewhere he didn't want to go. Looking back now I know that was a mistake. Later that night he called me back. He didn't call to say he was feeling suicidal but was okay. It did make me feel a little better knowing he was doing okay, but as I learned the next day he hadn't been doing better, at least not after the call to me. Thinking about those last days and moments of knowing him, I tried to piece it together the best I could why he had done it. Part of it was him just not telling me everything he had been feeling. Probably at times he wasn't definite he was going to do it, but finally made the decision after being by himself and feelings things wouldn't change for himself or just maybe thinking what ever was on the other side would be better or nonexistent. He at first did tell he had feeling suicidal, so he was reaching out and wanting to live and connect. Suicide is an attempt to end it all and an attempt to want to communicate or live also. During the brief time I had known him and thinking back at those times I can only guess at some of the factors. He by the time I had met him had developed issues of feeling like he had messed up his life and felt he had been a disappointment to his family. At times he just wanted to drive by or be around his parents. He felt a need to prove to his family that he wouldn't mess up, talking mostly about alcohol and drug abuse as I remember. He had been trying to find a way to feel approval from them in some way, whether they knew that or if that was the way he perceived the situation. I would never know. I never did talk to his parents about the suicide or knowing him. I seen them at the visitation and a few times briefly since the funeral but haven't had any contact with them. I'm not really sure what I would say. I mostly had some guilt feelings of not being able to stop it, not putting him in the hospital the day before he died. He said he once asked if they had knew me and they stated they didn't. They didn't connect me to my Dad at that time. Going to the visitation and seeing him laying the coffin, I just wanted to avoid the family. I don't know how they would of reacted, would they be angry for me letting him stay in his apartment. I know I heard his Dad was upset with the store letting him purchase a gun that day, but didn't hear anymore about anything after that. That last phone call the night before he had died was him talking about how everything seemed to going okay with them, they were in a good mood when he had called. Looking back he seemed to take it more as they didn't care. He was feeling bad and wanted something from them but didn't or wasn't able to get it, or he had felt that way. I just seen a little of what his issues were, how much they affected the end I don't know, or even what I perceived is correct, but those were perceptions and thoughts at the time.

After John had died it was hard having to go back to work and being around the apartment site. The other individuals who lived there, were already susceptible to depression, some responding with some anger, with the sense of loss and reasons for more despair in their lives at that time. One of the individuals who was living there, was gone visiting family when John had died. They had came back a few days after, and I was working the night they were coming back. The person had a brother commit suicide when they were younger, and she had a history of attempts in her life. I had the responsibility to let her know what had happened and to make sure she would be okay and safe. She had a pretty hard time with it, eventually becoming near a catatonic stage of not being able to be responsive. She wasn't left alone that night. It

---

was a draining period of time for a while. She seemed to recover briefly after that night, and things seemed to be going okay or at least that what it seemed.

One night later she was making vague good-bye statements, being in a good happy mood. At the time she was saying those statements I didn't quite catch on to what she was meaning or talking about for sure, but it caught my attention, or at least causing some confusion. In hindsight I don't know why I didn't be more direct with her about what she was talking about or wanting to do. I suppose I just left it alone to not create tension or not wanting to create a situation when there wasn't one. She wasn't depressed or appearing suicidal, so I just left it alone at the time. The next day she had appeared to have taken off. I was the first one to notice she wasn't there the next day, remembering those comments of yesterday. I contacted my supervisor immediately and we searched her apartment for any clue that might show up. I soon had found a letter she had written and left for us. She in the letter gave some indication she might try to kill herself, but it was vague and she didn't know if she would or not. In the meantime, trying to find where she had gone, and whether she would kill herself, I was reliving those last moments of contact with her, however brief, and what I should of or shouldn't of done. Wondering whether she would safe and be back. I think that's the hard part about suicide, you can't control someone or be responsible for someone's actions but usually when someone dies from suicide there are signs and images in your head that you can see that point to that decision of suicide. Part of me was angry with her for putting myself and others through this again and another part was dealing with the guilty feelings of not doing enough to stop it before it went as far as it had. She communicated some of her intentions but not clearly, but clear enough to see the pattern looking back. That's part of the clues, they do catch your attention, but you don't always know the best way to act on them or whether just not to act on them at all.

She ended up not harming herself and was found that she was safe. She had a friend pick her up and she went to another city, but didn't tell anyone of her intentions beside she might hurt herself. She ended up moving from the apartment complex. For awhile I was over cautious, not wanting something bad to happen again.

Things settled down for awhile, a year or so then another incident happened out of the blue. It was at the same apartment site with an individual who had known John. Probably part of it was easier for him to attempt because of the past incident with John. Suicide is usually in some way an attempt to communicate something they can't fully convey, a cry for help, or just a cry of wanting things to end instead of feeling and going through their pain, just not having the energy to deal with it anymore. With the past incident in the person's mind, it somehow seems more acceptable or a pattern to follow on some level.

The incident started out just like any day. I had taken the individual to the store to get some items and had dropped him off. There wasn't really anything different from past days. He like John was always dealing with some frustrations of not having his life being like he had envisioned before being diagnosed with an mental illness. His plans were interrupted with needing to be put in a hospital, that he felt he didn't need or want to be in. He was always struggling with not being able to have or keep a job. Feeling the disappointment from his parents of who he was. Having the past history of drug abuse and irresponsible behavior labeled to him, either by himself or others. Even through it had been twenty-five years since that first hospitalization he seemed to relive that day in his mind almost everyday. Working through the grief of what could of been, or fighting with the concept he didn't have a mental illness. The day I took him to the store, he was probably more quiet than usual, but still had the underlining tension and frustration of his life, lined with anger and disappointment. That time he didn't discuss those feelings of his past when he was with me, he just seemed angry and got out of the van and went up to his apartment. A few minutes later after dropping him off, he took a bunch of pills and got scared and quickly found someone to tell, and was immediately taken to the hospital. I met them at the hospital and seen him go into a semi-conscious state and then he went to a complete unconscious state when we were trying to talk to him to keep him awake. It was kind of a helpless feeling of seeing someone go unresponsive and not being able to do anything. The overdose was taking an affect, and they started pumping his stomach, and he got the needed medical help he needed. He spent a few days in the hospital and came back to his apartment. He didn't want to die that day, just wanting to communicate his pain and grief of his life, with that split moment of thinking it would just be easier to end it all. It didn't end that way and he still struggles with the grief of his life, but deals with it the best he can. Having good and bad days with overtime being able to accept who he is and being okay where he is with his life and being able to grow and regain that joy for life at times.

My brother Jason also had contact with other people the day he died. He had wanted to take the day off from school and wanted someone to take the day off. He didn't communicate to anyone how he was feeling, and he wasn't able to find someone to take the day off with him, so he became feeling more alienated and alone. He on some level wanted to be connected to others, but when he felt he wasn't able to communicate his feelings or have an outlet, he at that particular moment just wanted to end those intense feelings he was having. I think a suicidal person wants someone to know how they are feeling, but when they don't, they feel more alienated and alone in their struggles. Sometimes individuals will do it near or in front of others, such as drug overdoses, wanting them to pay attention or wanting others to know of their pain, or a form of revenge to get back to cause them pain in some form. Sometimes it's just a quick snap reaction of anger, disappointment, hopelessness that can and does pass if they are able to find other ways of dealing with it. It can also be dealing with prolonged depression and frustrations of events of their life's that go unresolved. You just don't know when there will be that increased spike that will push the edge enough to make an attempt, but it can always be there in a person that hasn't developed healthy coping skills or preventive measures.

Another individual that I just had just started to get to know, came into the office of where I was working one evening. The individual hadn't been there long before he made an attempt. He came into the office, wanting something. I don't even remember what for, but not anything to deal with wanting to kill himself. He wanted something I didn't have or couldn't do for him. Soon after that he took a bunch of pills surrounded by others in their apartment. Don't really know if the events were related or not, beside the short time sequence in between. An ambulance was called and he would be okay, but that wasn't known at the time. His attempts appeared more out of immaturity or impulse, but I never really got to know him that well. Years later I met his Mom and she talked briefly about him, dealing with the frustrations of him being in a hospital or institution and not being able to be home. That is the cycle for some people, going in and out of places, not being able to develop healthy coping mechanisms or stable stability. Suicide awareness and prevention involves knowing and understanding the effects of suicide and attempts on others and the self, building awareness of yourself and what you are experiencing and how to deal with those feelings in a healthy way. Learning skills not just to survive but to enrich someone's life. A lot of times there just isn't a lot of discussion or awareness of why someone makes an attempt, healing doesn't take place, just the stigma and more depression from the attempts.

Another part of suicide at times is the attempt of wanting to punish or revenge factor that the individual is feeling. I had started working with an individual in their apartment, when another person, who was a past friend of theirs needed a place to stay and was staying at the apartment for the time being. They previously had support services and wanted to try to regain supports, but at the time wasn't able to get because of some past negative history and legal issues. The person couldn't live at the apartment site and would eventually have to move. One night I came to work with the person who was living there, and this person who was wanting services was expressing some frustrations and angry feelings toward others, stating how you guys will be sorry as I walked out of the apartment. The comment caught my attention and made me feel uncomfortable, because it had been somewhat tense with her being there, I was in the middle of something I didn't really have any control of and not really being able to do anything about it. I was just mainly wanting to get out of the apartment and finish the services. The next time I came back to the apartment it was early evening the next day. A couple of individuals wanted me to check on her. She was laying on the couch in her nightgown on. She had a pale color to her, and was breathing irregularly and deeply. She had saliva coming out of her mouth, drooling. I immediately called 911 for an ambulance, talking to them as they were coming. It didn't take long for them to come, but it seemed to be long time as I was waiting and talking to the 911 operator. I got someone to help me turn her to the side so she wouldn't choke on her saliva. Her night gown was slipping off and she was naked underneath, just what appeared at the time a person close to end of a life. I quickly got her robe on her and waited for the ambulance. They soon got there and took her to the hospital. At the time the hospital wasn't sure if it was a suicidal attempt or some physical problem. At the hospital they made everyone put a mask over their face who was near her. I remembered those remarks of you guys will be sorry as I left, but at time I didn't really think of suicide. It would became clearer after seeing her laying there. I had to make out a report for police, but my mind was scattered and rattled, I couldn't remember my current phone number but for some reason I could remember a former number and just put that down. She ended up being transferred to a larger hospital and after a while she fully recovered and was grateful she didn't die. She did it around people in part I suppose because she didn't really want to die. She appeared to do it in part because of anger or revenge intertwined with despair. "Unsuccessful attempts" at least relieves some of the agony of the event. You don't have to deal with grief of death, but it sets up alarms that something is wrong or needs attended to in some way. The person or others may be ashamed of the event. Sometimes the cycle is over and other times the cycle is started or continued again when situations arise in their lives, whether it is a month or years down the road. The person at times still needs to look at what happened and heal and learn from it. That doesn't always happen although and the same themes and patterns can come up again.

With completed suicides, the end is the end of a physical life ending in sadness. The cycling is over and completed. What stands is dealing with the finality of it all and the legacy of the person not being able to cope with themselves and life. Barb was another one of those individuals that I had started to get to know. She had a mental illness, where she had difficulty wanting to be outside of her house. When I went out with her she seemed to do fine, but she felt it was an issue with her. That she needed that support or encouragement to do it, to get out of the house and do needed tasks. Well she went through a time where she kept canceling and not getting out of her house, stating she was too weak or ill. She was becoming more paranoid and distraught over a relationship she was having at the time. She soon after that was found in her apartment, where she had hung herself. When I heard the news it did catch me by surprise, but I knew she wasn't doing well at the time. I just wanted to spent time by myself after hearing it, not really want to deal with another person who didn't want to live. I went to a nearby mall by myself, and went shopping for some new clothes and watched others in the mall walking around enjoying themselves. I just wanted to be around people who enjoyed life and didn't want to die. It took a little while before anything was written in the paper. It seemed almost liked it never happened. That's the thing with suicide at times, it never gets discussed and life moves on. There was a nice obituary written by her family and a service for her, in which I didn't go to, just using the excuse I had to work. Part of me felt that I and or the "system" had failed her in some way. No one really is to be blamed or judged for suicide, but I think you should still look at the situation to see if there is anything that can be learned or taken from it. Sometimes it feels that isn't the case. She had a mental illness that clouded her thinking and feelings but at the same time she was a very intelligent warm individual trying to cope day to day.

Depression, Mental Illness, and ADHD

Healthy people don't commit suicide is a statement that I first read about suicide. At first I took some disagreement to it, even through it reads as common sense. At first reading it I had taken it as somehow the statement was saying my brother Jason was somehow defective in some way, not validating the importance of who he was and just labeling him in a category. People are never just there illness or disorder. They may have a disorder or illness but it doesn't define who the person is. Knowing that a person is dealing with an issue that can contribute to suicide does help contribute to some understanding and less judgment by others and themselves. But with any disorder or illness it may take time and knowledge of how it is affecting you so you can do something about it. If you don't realize you have something physical going on contributing, you don't know how to deal with what is going on, and why it is happening. When the pain exceeds the coping skills to deal with everyday life, the balance is out of whack and the risk of suicide is greater. With some form of chemical balance going on, thought processes can get distorted, losing sight of what got you to the point of suicidal feelings because they become so intensified.

I had a friend in college that I had known during my junior year and senior years. During the time I didn't really connect with what was going on with him and he didn't either. A lot of times mental illness will start to show up during the college years. There will be some kind of change and the person deals with something for the first time not really knowing what is happening. For him the change was from always having an over abundance of energy and feeling good to feeling down in the dumps for no apparent reason. He was just down all the time, and he couldn't point out anything that had specific caused him to feel that way. He just couldn't pull himself up and was losing confidence in himself and felt he couldn't ask help from a professional. It was a complete change from the way he had been, and he was draining the people around him with his feelings of depression. I had on and off connection with him, but one day I seen him in the store toward the end of the school year and he said he was feeling so much better and back to his former self and left smiling. I ended up graduating a short time after that and haven't seen him again. After working a few years in the mental health system I thought how he fit the classic bipolar disorder, I don't know for sure but he had the symptoms and behaviors of it. Looking back I just wondered what happened to him and if he continued to cycle and how he was doing. Part of that was disappointing to me because I was a psychology major in college and at the time a mental illness was something that never occurred me. I was just thinking he was going through a hard time and should be able to pull himself out of it. If he would only look at things in a positive way or do things to pull himself up. That's probably one of the hardest aspects of mental illness, seeing your loved one changed into another person or not being able to do things they used to. Not that the person can't be successful and live a good life but it helps if they are aware of what's happening and willing to do the things that keep themselves healthy.

My brother Jason was never diagnosed with anything particular, but during the readings he said he had something like Attention deficit disorder which led himself to be more impulsive and difficulty with concentrating and memory which was a contributing factor to the way he had been feeling and acting toward the end.

How you look at life contributes to how you feel about yourself. Depression causes you to look at life as hopeless and not worth living. I had found a student pass of Jason's, in which he had written on the back of it with names of people in different categories, friends, and girls he had liked. There were a list of thirty eight males he considered a friend and twenty seven female friends, and another four he was attracted to. Sometime during the year he had died he had written down those names of friends but at the end his world would become so small he had forgotten or he could no longer feel his friends and family. He was only sixteen but couldn't see a future for himself. That's what depression can do to you and your thinking. It gives you a lack of energy to find an solution and to deal with anything anymore. The Attention deficit with the combination of feeling depressed, isolated, drinking alcohol and not feeling he would have what he wanted in his life contributed to the end. It was just a combination of factors, events of the day and lack of impulse control clouded more by alcohol that contributed the unhealthy mind set he was feeling and thinking. That's the thing with stopping yourself from suicidal actions, being able to endure that wave of acting on those feelings and letting them pass until you can think more rationally and healthy. My brother didn't really know what was going on within himself or why it was happening. If I remember right he had a doctor appointment the day he had died. I don't know if it would of changed anything or not. I think my Mom felt there was something just not quite right with what was going on with him, and my Dad thought more of he was just going to be okay and it would pass. That's the thing with hindsight with suicide, wondering and looking back at the past that was. With mental illness or any disorder sometimes it takes years before it is correctly diagnosed or even if it is, the person can't accept it or do the things to keep themselves healthy. Areas that seem to be the hardest at times to change is having to take meds, not drinking alcohol, recognizing unhealthy thinking and actions. I went through a brief time of taking a few individuals to AA meetings and just sat and listened to the individuals in the meeting. One of the individuals who shared his story talked about having a mental illness, sharing how he would be in the middle of a street shouting in a paranoid state, with the police talking to him trying to get the situation under control. He during the AA meeting could see how his mental illness affected him and some of the grief it had caused him during acute episodes. He seemed rational and sincere at the time of the meeting dealing with his illness. He came across sincere, and had some awareness of how his illness affected him and was trying to deal with it in healthy ways, not drinking, attending meetings and openly discussing his issues with others. The other people at the meeting, including myself felt compassion and admiration for him and his attempts for recovery. A few years later he made the local paper. He was back in one of the those paranoid states and had shot one of his neighbors. He didn't kill him, but there was a trial involved and he got the needed help he needed. It kind of made me sad thinking of what others were probably thinking of him and the grief of his illness continuing. I'm not really sure where he ended up but did see him a few years later back with his family. The norm for a person with a mental illness is not to become harmful to others, but it does happen and creates even more of that stigma for a person who has mental illness. Mental illness can flare up like any physical illness, if you don't take of yourself or get the help needed it can cause problems for the individual. It doesn't happen in every case, but more than often a person with mental illness lose their family, their kids, spouses and family members because of the impact, conflicts and issues with mental health issues. They have to deal with the grief of having a mental illness and the grief of losing family members and support. Mental illness at times goes through cycles, there are times where your doing well and times that your are not doing well, just like any one else, but sometimes the cycles are more extreme or unhealthy. Everyone is different in the way they cope. Some do well and remain stable, others cycle at different levels, than their are some that can transcend their illness and can inspire others. Mental illness doesn't have to define the person or their life, but you have to become aware of how your thought processes work, and be able to step aside from them and see how they are affecting you and others, and whether they are real or imagined.

Looking for a Missing Person

I first heard the news of Kate missing as I turned into the parking lot of my office building, meeting the co-worker who was the last one who had seen her. She said she had seen her and tried to talk to her or just say hi, but Kate appeared to just want to avoid her and be on her way. That one moment in time that stands in time for those who experience it. She told me that Kate had been missing since that last moment. Her missing had been put in the paper, so there was a citywide search being put together starting at the local town square. It seemed to be happening so fast. From things being normal to chaos. I could only think about the last time I had seen and talked to her. It was a couple of weeks before hearing she was missing. She was at the town square listening to a music concert with friends. Now we were gathering at the town square to look for her. I was glad to be able to see her those few weeks before, wanting to be there for her more than I had. I had wanted to take the opportunity to sit down with her on the ground and catch up on how she was doing. Little did I know at the time it would be the last time. She appeared she was doing well, a little less stressed out than previous times I had seen her. I brought up to her how she looked like she was losing weight again and she acknowledged how she was needing to go back to the doctors for a checkup and was fearing that her cancer was coming back. As she was going through cancer she would have periods of losing or gaining weight depending upon how the cancer was progressing. Even with the weight loss she seemed back to her old self that I had known. She a few times had went through periods of what was almost in a manic stage, trying to cope and deal with the issues in her life. Her life seemed to be hit with one thing after another the last few years. Relationship issues at home, dealing with a divorce and dealing with the court in regards to custody of her child with her ex-husband. Her mother also recently passing away a few months ago. She had been co-worker of mine when I first starting working in the community about twelve years ago. She was one of the few co-workers that had been around since I started working in the mental health field. She had been through other people's suicide attempts and completions the same way as I had. She had experienced dealing with individuals who repeatedly would feel suicidal or make threats, and she was the first person I called when I heard my brother had killed himself. It is a vivid as the day it had happened, that phone call. She had a son that was about Jason's age and had known each other. She had just recently talked to me about her son knowing Jason. Over the years she became not only a co-worker, and supervisor but a good friend and an advocate for myself and others. She had helped me through a rocky period in a relationship, and advocated for me at my job like she had for so many people she had come in contact with in her life. She had became my supervisor and one of my guides in dealing with those affected by mental illness and depression. Her young son had a disability and she was always fighting for the best possible education and supports for him while she was going through all of her own personal struggles. She had been on this side, knowing what it is like when someone dies from suicide, or the just the stress and apprehensive when someone becomes suicidal. She had been through it just like I had, so when I first heard she was missing and possibly suicidal it was something that I wasn't quite prepared for or wanted to be prepared for. If she was taking this path, could I also take this path at some point? Everyone has a breaking point, what events would it take me to go this way? Would I do the same thing in her position? What had all of those experiences of the past mean now? How would it effect those past individuals who she tried to help in their suicidal moments. How would it effect me if she killed herself? Did she think about those past experiences? How did those past experiences of dealing with suicidal and depressive individuals effect her thinking if any. When I first heard she had been missing I thought things might be okay, thinking she just needed to get away from things and be by her self, since she had been having a lot of stress in her life. As the details emerged that sense of things would be okay became more tentative apprehensive, knowing that I had been here before.The last few years had been hard on Kate and things just seem to come right after another for her.When I first started working with Kate,when she first became my supervisor she was at the top of her game. She was good at what she did and enjoyed her job.We had a small knit group at work and worked together through the battles we faced on the job,but as the company grew,it became more separated into separate parts because it became larger,where Kate had felt she had less control.Not that the program and services didn't become better,it was just growing and changing with new and younger people coming over and taking over what once was Kate's, at least that was her perception and feeling. She in a sort of joking way but a serious way stated she felt like the first Star Trek series,her being the first generation and having the new generations coming in,pushing her to the side. I think she used that analogy because she knew I had liked Star Trek and was amused by that. I soon had put a picture of the original cast, Captain Kirk, Spock and the Doctor on her wall with another poster I had gotten that had statements of how I've learned everything I know about life from Star Trek. She was amused by the poster and the pictures, but it did in some way characterize what it is like to get older and stay in the same job for awhile. Not that Kate was old, but experiences and people come and go. Sometimes those experience and knowledge just seem to be lost with the new and possibly perceived brighter future with lack of felt acknowledgment or validation of who and what became before. Life always moves forward it seems. Kate had started for awhile feeling she had lost her place and identity at work. She was having increased agitation at work and had quit briefly before she found out she had cancer. She later recognized later she was having a hard time at work in part because of the cancer, or at least it was another part of the equation of her quitting work.

She was unemployed, quit the job she once loved, feeling that loss of her role and esteem that it brought, going through a divorce and custody issues, fighting cancer, and the death of her mother intermixed with mental health issues with herself and the father of her other child. She just had a lot of things going on at the same time, and had been out of work for a couple of years due to her health. Bills were piling up and the feeling that her cancer was coming back.

At that time she had been seen at the local drugstore she was in her plan of action of ending her life. She was on her final walk of her life. There were news reports on the local news stations. It seemed kind of surreal having a part of your surroundings or past and present on TV. After hearing about Kate missing, later that evening I went to the square where they were gathered to meet to start looking for Kate around the area. The report was she was last seen around the local Drugtown store. She was on foot walking since her car was still at her house. Her boyfriend had talked to her briefly on her cell phone. She making some indications she had taken some pills. The cell phone went dead,there was some noise of a plane and a train. So that was the indications of where she might be or ended up. The cell phone signal could only give a certain range that in was within a couple mile range in or around the town, At the square, the plan was to take the town into sections, walking around different areas all around the town. The police had already looked along the railroad tracks with a plane and on the ground with dogs, but came up with nothing. I and another person took off walking. We had all broken up into small groups. We were suppose to look into abandoned places, garages, or anywhere someone could hide or be hidden from sight possibly. At first I just tried to stay casual and trying not to show too much concern, hoping I wouldn't really finding her laying dead somewhere. At the same time hoping to find her okay, and her just needing to get away for a short time. We could just give her a hard time, joking how the town had gathered looking for her. Part of me was holding my feelings in, hoping the best would occur, knowing it probably wouldn't be. Not really wanting to feel any thing particular yet until I knew how I should. I looked into a dumpster with apprehension wondering if this was really happening or what I needed do. Along the first search, I ran into an individual who was also searching for Kate. He was one of the individuals who on several occasions in the past had felt like just wanting to die and have his life end. Kate had been on the end of those calls on more than one occasion. I noticed him and went over to talk to him. He was in the process of looking for Kate on his bicycle. The emotions of seeing him at that moment was of concern, not knowing what or how it would effect him and others who had been suicidal in the past. He seemed fine and just wanted to help if he could. He was searching just like everyone else. At least on the outside he appeared to be dealing with it okay. He I suppose knew what it was like to want to die and didn't judge the situation or Kate. He also didn't know at the time what was actually happening beside Kate was missing. I made my first tour or section of the town, looking in garages, dumpsters, and just any place where someone may be where someone maybe could hide for a brief time. Nothing came about, so we went back to the square to see if there was any more news of Kate's whereabouts. That nervous energy of wanting to know something but not yet knowing how to feel. Took a break, got something to drink, and made plans to visit another area of the town where she might of been or gone at some point. We took off to the side of the town where she might of walked if she had continued walking further and where the clues might indicate. We went to the edge of the town, where there was a recreational walking path along the edge of a golf driving area. There were a few individuals teeing off on the driving range, just like any day, practicing their golf swings. It was kind of strange and stressful. Normalcy intertwined with a crisis that was happening. Before we began, we were told part of it was already searched, along the path trails, so at least at the beginning I didn't search that close to the walking path. As we began, we heard a plane taking off, the airport was not that far away. It kind of gave me an eerie feeling that this might be the place. Part of me wanted to be able to find her so it would at least be over, the other part I didn't want to find her and have that last image of her laying dead on the ground. Trying to stay calm and relaxed, just kind of going through the steps of looking for her without knowing or what emotions to feel. Not wanting to get upset because I didn't know how I should be feeling. At the beginning of the search in that area, I ended up skipping a part of it, searching far away from the trail pathways, remembering they had already searched that area. Part of me wanted to search that particular area that I had passed. The other part or voice in my head said you don't need to search that area. I just bypassed the area. I ended up searching a lot of the area, beside the beginning. We went back to square, part of me was relieved I didn't find her, the other part I was hoping it would be over so I would know something and hoping things could be okay. Nothing was found and there was no more news. I decided I had enough and just wanted to get away by myself, but I ended up going over another by myself. Part of me was still scared of actually finding her, with now some angry feelings creepy up inside of me, thinking how she was doing this to me. Why would she go missing and making implications of ending her life this way, after she herself had been through similar incidents of those wanting to die. I searched through an area where there were old train cars. I wasn't able to get into the train cars, only looking through the windows when available. Nothing was found so I just headed home and called it an evening.

The next day the search continued, I went out again after work, trying to piece together the events and clues. Thinking what path and steps Kate might of taken after being last heard of. I took a brief walk to the side of town where Kate might of walked then headed back to my office at work after not finding anything. That is when I knew something had happened. The co-worker who had last seen her was just getting off of the phone, and she was crying. At that moment I knew she had been found. She was found laying in the area I had searched, the area near the walking path where the golfers were hitting balls at the golf range. I'm not sure the exact spot but I would bet it was in the area I went by going with the thoughts that went through my head of whether I should go check that area more. It sounded like the area I had previous been but had skipped part of it, thinking of she probably wouldn't be there. There was a larger search in that area, with several people going through that area at one time sweeping the area. The clues all had led to the area, and that was where she had been found. It had rained overnight, and from what I heard from the person who had found her, her body was okay, looking like she just laid down to rest. I then received a few phone calls telling me they had found her, telling them I just heard also. I caught up with the person who I had ran into previous, who had in the past several suicidal moments, letting them know she had been found, and that she had passed. He seemed okay with it, not getting upset, appearing to take it okay, but knowing it was a sad moment. I'm not really sure what he thought, but he has seemed to deal with it and accept it as it was. I at that point still didn't know what I should or want to feel about it. The next day at work we had scheduled all staff training, it was changed to talk about the issues of Kate's death and her suicide. I should of expected that, but wasn't yet ready to talk about or just really didn't want to. My first reaction and continual reaction was just to leave the meeting and be by myself, in some way protesting the situation. I knew I had to stay seated in the chair and make it through the discussions because I knew I couldn't hide from it. I sat and listened. I seemed to just grow more angry, mostly just at Kate for the way she had passed. I was wondering how others who had affected by suicidal thoughts would cope and deal with the news. In the room there was another individual who I had previously written about who had a suicide attempt and who had been going through cancer at the same time as Kate's. He was doing okay with the cancer, he also had apprehension about his cancer coming back also. The tension of wondering how he would deal with her death and his own cancer was something that was there, you didn't know how to deal with, wondering if he would just quit also. The following days, there were days he would come into the office talking about or briefly stating comments about suicide. I could tell he was or had been processing aspects of suicide and it wasn't something he would do presently but it was definitely apart of his thinking. That heavy energy of thoughts that hang in the air but not fully discussed for whatever reason. My initial thoughts of anger or frustration had stayed with me during the meeting. I had made statements to myself of not attending the funeral due to them and somehow protesting the way she had decided to pass. In some way it had felt like a slap in the face. I ended up talking some to a friend and the therapist who had ran the discussion group in regards to Kate's death. That seemed to help some and realize I didn't want to or need to remain angry with her. I attended the funeral and realized I just wanted to appreciate being a part of her life. There were pictures of her at the funeral of her life, seeing her in moments that I hadn't known her, or just all of those moments where she was so full of life and happy. I felt appreciative of just having the opportunity of knowing her and at least a part of her experiences while she was here. I knew Kate's had been going through difficult times, it just wasn't the difficult times, but her mental health wasn't the same as it had before. I remember seeing in the eyes of people who didn't really know her until toward the end, when hearing her name, you could see the tension or the eyes roll up, thinking she is hard to deal with. In fact, toward the end she was, her mental state was a little out of whack. Her emotions and thoughts were at times out of whack. I think she knew that at times, other times she was okay. That's the thing about a chemical imbalance of the mind, it's hard to stop what the brain is perceiving and acting, dealing with emotions, loops of thoughts and being able to step outside of the illness when your not doing well or balanced. That is the same for any kind of situation or intense emotions or out of a balanced mental health. Life can be full of drama and uncertainty just how to handle things. I didn't spend as much time I would of liked with Jason or Kate toward the end of their life's. You just think you have the time. One of my last memories of Jason I have is my Dad asking him to go down to the gas station to get some bread or milk for supper. Jason took off but didn't come back, not sure if he ever got the stuff. There was something strange about him not coming back, but it wasn't soon after that his suicide came about. The events were not related, just one of the events that kind of catches your attention, something isn't quite right but your not sure where to place it. The end of a life intertwined with the turmoil, confusion of various thoughts and behaviors of a person that is in turmoil. But life would move on.

I continued my search to see if I could find answers to any questions that might be answered. What would Kate say or be like if she was still "alive"? So I poked myself back to into the psychic world that remains hidden in my little world. The first attempt went to no avail. Kate didn't seem to be able to tune in or wasn't ready during the first reading, so it was rescheduled to a later time. This time I focused more on just Kate, mainly by just sending a picture of her I had to the psychic. It was the only picture of her I had, it wasn't a picture she particularly liked. She had sent it to me through email when we were playing around. Well it seemed to work, because Kate came through much clearer with her thoughts and personality. It was nice to be able to feel her energy in the room that I had known, even through it was a short time. It seems when your doing a reading it seems like you get that chance to talk to that personality and energy that you had known. Looking from a far it seems strange even writing about talking to mediums. The process may be different, you just take the information as it is and learn about it and what comes from it. Kate still didn't have all of the answers but she was on that path of understanding how our thoughts and perceptions impact ourselves and our own world, including our health. She brought up the words of suicide and cancer. She couldn't tell me what her suicide meant, she said it was up to myself and my individual perceptions to define what it meant to me. She I think didn't know yet what to think of it, it was just what it was, the end of a life. She was just ready to go on to the next world of unknowns on her terms instead of the cancer terms. She brought up the term cancer and the impact it had had on her. She brought up how she didn't want to continue to go through treatments and having others having to deal with the decline of her health. She then brought up how she knew how her cancer had started in the first place, or at least one of the strong factors. That was the belief that was related to her marriage and divorce. Her words were that "bitch",referring to the female that her husband had been cheating with during the marriage. That was a big focal area for Kate while here. She was frequently talking about her husband cheating on her, and it still remained during the reading. The belief that she wasn't attractive or good enough, and those angry feelings toward her husband and the "other woman". The time she was first diagnosed with cancer was intertwined with the chaos of the end of her marriage.

Probably the chaos of the end of the marriage intertwined with the belief of not feeling attractive or good enough during a lifespan, which peeked toward the end helped create the framework of cancer. She said the cancer started with that belief of not feeling attractive or good enough. She said here is only different because of a different focus. Here thoughts or beliefs impact much faster, so you can see it more quickly. In the physical things are more slower and denser, but have the same impact over a period of time. She went on to various philosophical thoughts, such as how young kids will think someone is gone if they can't be seen, such as a hide and seek game. The child thinks the person is gone if they are behind the door and can't understand that they are just in the other room or on the other side of the door. Correlating that to the belief of death, if you can't see or hear, such as using the senses of eyes and ears and touch the person, they don't exist. The child is at a certain place, where they need to be and are and will grow and learn. That is the same for any age or person, they are where they need to be or where their understanding is and that's okay.

Kate was described being in the bar, with her beer buddies talking philosophy of life. If I had one perception of what her life might be like now if she was "alive' that would be the image. It brought a smile to my day, thinking that some things stay the same, whether your here or there. At least part of what it may be like if life continues. As before I guess it doesn't really matter whether Kate was there or not, it was good to talk about and discuss issues of life that matter or ponder upon. Kate didn't finish all of her physical struggles like my Dad had done, so part of that makes her death seem premature and still not a complete ending in grace somehow. Kate at times was going through periods of dealing with mental health issues which influenced her decision at the end. As said before healthy people don't commit suicide as a general rule. Healthy meaning in spirit and the mind. She left three kids behind, wondering how they fit in at the end, and what paths they might encounter in their futures. As in any suicide there are an array of emotions and reactions to it. You have the reality and loss of a life, entangled with the perception of life shortened prematurely.

Conclusions So Far

My hope some day would be that we would know if we are more than just a body. To kill the body, kill the struggle, kill the emotions of pain, despair, anger, hopelessness or whatever ales the mind and body at the time, with the hope of ending it all. To know if it does go completely away with a single action. I've sifted through some of the thoughts that may go into making of a suicide, but I think to fully grasp what it may be like is wonder what it may be like during those last few moments of a suicide. That leap to pull that trigger just a inch, to digest those pills and wait to see what happens. To feel the rope around your neck tighten. Placing yourself in that situation, feeling that gap of wanting to live and wanting to die. Whatever is between that gap that creates that action is where thoughts are to live and die. I can't say over the years, I haven't wanted to focus or needed to focus on those last few seconds of my brother's life. Trying to place myself in that situation on that gravel road with him reminds me the need to do something. I wished I could of just gave him a big hug and a cry to somehow bring him back before it all happened. To have a body but more than such a thing that goes away into the wind of ashes at the end. That is the question. Are we spiritual beings or just hollow flesh and bone or both.

I seen in the paper a young man of twenty three that had killed himself. For whatever reason it doesn't really seem to matter at the time of sorrow what his story is about. It just seems the same story, if I kill myself, my body then I can end it all, the suffering, the anticipation of suffering. The day to day life struggles, the frustration of being in the place that you are currently in or dealt. The story of that young man does matter although. He was here, he was somebody to someone. He had a path to follow, a life to lead.

He was the same age that Jason would be now if he had lived. He was a former classmate of Jason's leaving myself wondering of how much he had known Jason and whether Jason was looking over the situation and how he was feeling about the new happenings in the air. Just another story stuck in the air that will pass. He wasn't anyone who that I had known. He was just another statistic of someone killing themselves for whatever reason. A life fully in front of him, gone by in the instance of his own action. Sometimes you can just see the patterns and know there is a high probability that they will lead to the path of self-destruction and you can't stop it.

After the time that has gone by since my brother had passed I would of hoped something would of changed, but it doesn't really, or change just seems to happen to slowly. People think they can still solve their problems if you they didn't exist. I wish I could somehow waive a magic wand and wake up and see that things will change instantly. For some I know it will change, for others the path will be chosen that fills me with empathy for the road they will and might travel, but knowing that is their path, in which I can not judge or change, only try to nudge whoever I come upon to that path of least destruction. Sometimes it just is and it is their time or the experience they need to go through. I can only pray for and give me my good will. We at times need to take time to nourish our spiritual side of ourselves in whatever form that may come in.

This year marked the twelve year anniversary of John's death. So on April 1st myself and another person went to John's grave to visit and drop off some flowers at his grave side for remembrance of him and his last moments here. There were still unanswered questions in the air between the two of those of how those last few hours of his life had played out. Questions that had carried with us both during these last twelve years that she had always wanted to know more about or just having some anger or frustrations toward John not being put in the hospital. She was the one that was with John, who encouraged him to seek help for his feelings of being suicidal. She was the one he went back to when he didn't go to the hospital. She was the last one to see him that night, before he had chosen his path. She told me, she just didn't know what to do after he came back to visit her that night. She had assumed that he would be put in the hospital and be in a safe place for the time being. When she heard the news the next morning that he had killed himself with a gun he had bought at the store, she was distraught and angry, and frustrated with the whole mental health system and it's people. She was mad at his doctors, different supervisors, but she never got or stated angry feelings toward me. She told me she wanted to ask me about those last moments I had been with him and why I didn't put him in the hospital. She knew I had contacted my supervisor on what to do, so she redirected her anger toward those in "authority". We ended up discussing what John had told her and what he had told me. What he had told me and what he had told her were different in regarding the intensity of how he was feeling. He had told her he had tried earlier to go to a store and purchase a gun, but was denied because he had stated he had a mental illness. He was more open to expressing how sad he was feeling when he talked to her. He didn't mentioned a previous attempt to purchase a gun earlier, or expressing the intensity of his feelings, probably looking back because he didn't want to be in the hospital, or he had enough of a plan already and wanted to avoid being stopped. Looking back now, and from experience if a person makes suicidal remarks they are just taken to ER to be evaluated by a doctor, not leaving it up to a judgment call. But even with that protocol that can be difficult, especially if the person doesn't have a previous mental health issues, such as my brother, and even if they do it can be a difficult and hard experience. I had attended an on call pager call where the person had stated they were feeling suicidal, then started saying they were not, just wanting to be left alone. So they locked themselves in their room, not wanting to come out. This person has a history of saying they were suicidal, so the police had to come and take her the hospital in chains for her own safety. After awhile in the ER and having the chains taken off of her, she decided she wanted to take off, because the doctor had concluded she needed to be hospitalized. She felt she just wanted to go back to her apartment and be left alone. She headed down the hall to start walking home and the police had to come after her and hold her down and put her in chains again. She eventually made it to the hospital but waiting for a long time in the ER, being cuffed for her own safety is something that happens often with mentally ill people. They get escorted by police in handcuffs like criminals in many way for their safety until they can come around to a more balanced state. Many people who have became suicidal often know of the routine of what to say or not to say to be hospitalized. Some want to be hospitalized and some don't. It is never an easy or comforting situation for any one involved.

I ended up showing her my brother's grave when we went to visit John's grave on his anniversary. He was buried in the same graveyard and told her he had committed suicide also. That was something she had not known. I at the time wasn't sure whether to show her or not, but decided to at the last moment. Many years after John's death those feelings and questions had remained. What could of been done? Why wasn't it done? Who is responsible, are others? Is it just the person who makes that final decision and takes that responsibility? Sometimes it just is. Sometimes something can be done, sometimes it plays out in whatever way you don't truly know why.

The only real conclusions I can come up with is that life can be rough. Its seems to go in cycles with the ups and downs along the way. For some those cycles are more harsh and unchanging with the desire and hope it can be ended with one single action of the hand.

It's just not that it can be hard, it's how you perceive things, how your mind is processing thoughts. I can't always give you the answers or feelings that you want to hear or feel. I don't know what your path and struggles are fully about. Why your path along this road is the way it seems it has to be. It may seem people don't get the same cards dealt to them, but everyone has their own challenges, strengths, and weakness. I could tell you that you live on past your death, hoping it would change your outlook but the choice is always up to you. In most cases you are not of clear mind, not being able to make wise choices. Anyone who commits suicide either does it to make an impact on others or feels that nobody will really care anyway. I've never seen that as true. There are always people that it affects, even if it is a stranger. The trick is to be able to recognize when you are not of clear mind and accept help or just being able to accept the time for the cycles to wane to a less harsh moment. I try not to judge you but I know of the pain that I wish not to endure. Life is life whatever path is chosen, it will continue. The scenery may change, but it still will be you watching it go by, whatever that awareness may be or come.

Sometimes you run in to people that it is fairly clear that they are on a path of self destruction, and you just feel helpless yourself in knowing how to reach them and get that breakthrough away from that path. Barry was one of the individuals. I only met him a few times but knew from the beginning I could tell how his life would unfold if things were not changed. He came to the center mainly to get a meal. Previously he stated he would scavenge the garbage cans for food, when he wasn't able to come up with money or food. He was a very intelligent person, but got in the cycle of depression that engulfed him and his being. He would get part time jobs at times doing handyman work, it was infrequent and not really knowing when they would come around. For him filing for disability and receiving a check from the government wasn't an option for him. So overall time he became in debt with rent, and bills, not being able to pay for periods of time. I don't really know his whole story, but like many people with some form of depression or mental illness, life can become fragile and seem overwhelming or not worth living. Barry recognized being depressed all the time stopped him from developing friendships or just losing the ones he did have. It became a cycle of his life. He wasn't feeling connected to his family anymore, he wasn't connecting to others because life had became too much of a hassle. This just wasn't the life he had planned or wanted, but he was in it, and he didn't know or belief he could get out of it. Meds weren't working, getting up in the morning was enough of a hassle for him. He would state, how could he be positive about his life or think things would change for him. Sometimes you just don't know how to reach someone, or what will reach him. I know Barry at times didn't want to be so negative about his life, but that just appeared to make him more depressed. When I heard he had killed himself, it wasn't much of a surprise, so this writing is my attempt at least to figure out a way to reach those people who think their struggles seem meaningless and no way out for them, beside ending it by their own hand. There are no easy answers to why life is so hard for some people. There is meaning or purpose to everyone's life, but for some they feel there isn't or they just can't find it for themselves and feel they can't climb out of what ever got them to the point of self-destruction. I'm not really sure what gives one person the fight to live and another one the fight to die. You can't really argue with someone who is feeling suicidal, they are feeling that way at the time. That is their world. That is how they perceive things. That is where their thoughts go. You can feel the despair in their souls. I still remember seeing him in the local store after a group meeting. The group had got on him somewhat for being negative about things. A few days later we caught eye contact, there still was that expression of his face showing sadness with a glim of guilt for being negative but not feeling able to pull himself out of it. Best you can do is guide them through and beyond those feelings of despair, thoughts and emotions. Let them know there is support and things they can do, whether it is just for a moment. Somewhere the person might gain awareness that they are here for a reason. There is a way out of what ails them. If only to accept where things are at that moment, and that is okay. What you do with life matters, not only to yourself but others. Many times the despair is from the perception that this is their life and the perception or thoughts that their life should of been this way or that way. Reconciling what could of been and what is. Being able to accept yourself and where your at in this moment. Suicide is aligned with thought disorders for many, recognizing that, may help a person recognize they need help and can be treatable. Life is full of so much more than despair and feeling suicidal. It's sometimes just a journey for some people to get there.

I wish you well along whatever journey you find yourself in, whether it will be completely blank for you, or be colored with life. At the end life will continue. It's really about life not death. To enjoy the moments of the day when they come.

My writing is based on two main areas, my life experiences, thoughts and perceptions and the belief that life continues in some general way after we leave our physical bodies. That belief is part based on hope that life does continue and what the "psychic" world is about. The perception that there is something more than the five senses. Part of the psychic part can just be confirmed by yourself, knowing what you already know, they just help confirm what is or has been happening. The other part of psychic world is being attuned to something that can't been seen with the eye or felt by the body. The psychic part is also based on perceptions, feelings, thoughts, intentions, emotions, and a connection to something bigger than yourself. Things you can't touch or see with the eyes, not only the outward expression and actions of a body. The spiritual part of your being. During the last year of my Dad's life, I just didn't know how to talk to him about what may happen after his death. I would go over at nights at times and just spend time with him, just checking to see how he was doing or if he needed anything. Visiting with him about his and my day or just watching TV. My Dad knew I had some belief in the afterlife because I had written him a story about Jason, but I never really talked to him about after death stuff. One night the TV show that came up was about the afterlife and what psychics thought. The show was on for about 15 minutes, but the whole time it was on, I acted like I didn't hear the TV, nor did I look at the it. Eventually he turned the channel. I wished I would of at least asked him during that brief time, what his belief was? What were his fears? What were his expectations and hopes? But I guess at that time he was also having the hope that he could survive through the lung cancer and I didn't want him or me to concede to death yet. I still wonder whether he wanted to talk about it or not, about what death met to him. I know from my experience from being with him and listening to him those final days, he was okay with dying. He was there when his Dad, Mom and brother had gone through the death process and was overall okay with the life he had led. We all face death at some point. It is somehow different when it is right in front of you. I knew he would be okay, and somehow wanted him to know he would be okay. But I think he knew that. I think he was looking forward to seeing Jason and being able to talk to him and heal finally from my brothers suicide, his son. I know he had the hope in that.

I suppose with suicide the person just wants a blank space, ending to it all, or at least not to have to deal with the current situations, an escape from it all. Can there be both? There are many different religions, many different beliefs. I could never tell someone what to believe, my writing is based upon some of my thoughts and perceptions. The Bible is based on many prophecies, psychic perceptions or hearing from what is perceived their GOD wanted. As you can see from the Old Testament to the New Testament, believes change. The Old Testament is harsher and the New Testament is of a lesser harsh. God didn't change but what people needed at the time changed. What they needed God to be changed. Beliefs usually fit the person or culture, that is probably one reason there are so many different beliefs. I think that is good and the way it should be. Life would be boring if we didn't have different cultures, ways of looking at life. You can believe that life ends at physical death, but it doesn't make it truth. A belief is not necessarily a truth. You could go on and on about beliefs and truths and opinions, hopes and faith. It just comes down to listening deep inside yourself and finding what life is about for you. Having faith in life.

Moving on or healing for myself was helped by the belief that we do live on and that I could and do have an ongoing connection to those who have crossed over to the unknown. When Jason died his energy or his connection to the physical was strong. Memories and his presence felt strong. Going over to my Dad and Moms houses I could feel his presence in just the physical belongings leftover. His clothes, his things in general were still there, just like he was just a short time ago, but now was gone. The physical surroundings and people who had been in his life remained.

I remember finding his car license and just wanting to hold on to that to keep a piece of him. I soon knew that I couldn't find Jason in physical things, so gave away the license. As time has passed the physical belongings that Jason left have seemed less attached to him and who he is now to me. They are just a small part of a time passed. I'm not to attached to looking for "signs" that he is around, maybe at the beginning but overtime life gets "busy" and moves on. Presence is felt in memories of thoughts, feelings and past experiences and now. Presence isn't felt in as much in grief and regret.

Two of his friends have named their kids after Jason. Those friends will always be a part of who Jason was and who he has become to me. I felt I had a connection in helping Jason in the healing process that he had to go through and is going through, like others in his life. The belief that we are all capable and are responsible for are own path, whether here or there and can learn from whatever path we decide to take helped me in my own healing process. Just knowing Jason and others have went down their own path, they were responsible for their own part of what got to them to their point. That's the only way they could really move on themselves and grow is to accept their own responsibilities for their choices. That they can and do grow and learn. They can and will experience good things and bad things, just like everyone.

As each anniversary goes by, things do move on. Life gets busy, daily responsibilities continue, happy and sad times continue. Some days are good, some days are not. Life goes on. I remember at the five year anniversary I was trying to hold unto a tree plant that I had gotten from work at Jason's funeral. I wasn't able to keep it alive much past that, but it really didn't bother me, since I'm such bad in growing plants anyway. But that plant signified something for me in some ways, because I did want to keep it alive, but couldn't. It had represented a small part of those memories when Jason had first died from suicide but I had to let it go.

Every so often I'm around the middle school, near the high school baseball field where they planted a tree and put a rock with his name on it for memorial. The area at times is full of busy activities. On one field, high school softball games are going on. On the other field, high school baseball games and a few people are playing on a nearby tennis court. Life continues. Parents enjoying watching their kid or friends playing sports, getting away from the business of the day and enjoying the day. Enjoying those moments when their kid is up to bat or catches a good hit. Fretting about the score of the game. Jason never played high school baseball, only making it to Babe

Ruth baseball, so in a way where it is, the high school ball fields signifies to what he missed out on, but also signifies some of the joy we had watching and being there when he was around. My daughter plays softball. I think of the joy it brings me being able to watch her. That first anniversary after Jason's death it was a little strange or sad going back to the ball park, but as time has passed it hasn't.

I had also went into a local grocery store and seen a can with a picture of a kid who committed suicide on that fifth anniversary, they were asking for money for something regarding the loss. He was from the same school that Jason had went to and passed away the same month as Jason had. It does and did give a sad feeling of another life ending in suicide and what that entails.

Just this week of writing, I became aware of an individual who had committed suicide because he was apparently headed to prison, leaving two young children behind. Their mother trying to help the kids understand the situation, friends wanting to be supportive. Just the start of all of the feelings of loss, pain and confusion of a suicide. Most people who commit suicide have the belief that they don't matter, or things just don't matter or not recognizing the sadness it can cause to others. I don't really know what that mother or kids need or will need. Everyone has what they need and their own path of healing and moving on. I think it is important to communicate to those who've passed on, not necessarily having to do through someone else. Just talking to them, letting out your feelings so you can heal and be heard, if only by yourself. From my experiences they will hear. Kate left young kids behind, who I know she truly loved, and this young man left young kids in the aftermath. What do you tell young kids and as they grow up, why their parent left?

When my daughter was about eight she needed to go to the doctor for having seizures. She hated the doctor and didn't want to go, she hated having seizures, or having someone talk to her about them. She was mad at missing school, feeling different or whatever and said she wished she was dead. I don't think she really knew at the time the impact of those words. Nothing more came from the incident, but it is something that stands out because of past experiences and the knowing of the impact of suicide and not wanting it to happen again. There still is some fear in situations when my daughter doesn't like who she is or where she is in her life as she approaches the teenage years and beyond.

Life is so busy it sometimes gets you distracted what is important and what is not. We are all important and connected in ways we may not even recognize. At times you do got to take the time to let others know how important they are to you for who they are. I don't really remember what happened on each anniversary anymore, but I do take time to remember each anniversary, birthday and how I'm and others are doing. At least taking account of where I'm at and what I have. I think there is a bigger picture of life and what and why we are here. We have earthly responsibilities and spiritual responsibilities or paths to lead. Sometimes we lose track of our spirit, the joy or happiness of life that it can bring. If I had to pinpoint one area that has helped me understand, heal and grow is through my own spirituality. The thoughts that go into believing there is something bigger than my individual ego that helps guide what is. That things happen for a reason. That there is support there during those hard times when we need it, and the believe that their can be awe and enjoyment in life. What one person needs for their spirit, may be different for each, but I think we all need soulful experiences and the belief that things happen for a reason. That we all have equal opportunities in finding and living that spirit. When at times we lose sight of our spirituality, that is when we just forget for those moments the awe of life and what it has to offer. Spirituality can come in many different forms, in the mundane of life, in different religions, in prayer, in thoughts and hopes of how life works and what death means.

Dancing with Death

Another aspect of suicide is understanding the path or choice a suicidal person chooses. Death means a way out of a current situation or a way out of future situations for a suicidal person. I'm not sure really how clear of a mind a person who is feeling suicidal is able to understand their choices they are making at the time, especially under severe stress and strain. In the young there is lack of experience, being in a place of just starting to find out who you are and finding who you want to become. With depression and other mental illness, there are periods where a person's thoughts and emotions can be out of balance and distorted, making it more difficult to make good decisions about their life's. Death may look like an ally or a friend to a person who wants to end it all. It becomes way of thinking or being. You began to have thoughts of wavering between life and those flickering control of inviting death. You may come to think you can choose when you want to dance with death, that's the intrigue of death of a suicidal mind. You invite it in as your friend, a way out. The core of suicidal thoughts is wanting to end the pain, what if death doesn't end the pain ?

So some questions regarding death are, is it the end of things, the turmoil, the thoughts and emotions that lead to the choice of death? It must be like jumping into the unknown, jumping off a bridge, where it just doesn't matter anymore where you will land, but hoping at the same time it will be better than where you are now. That last movement that you do, not knowing what will happen for sure, knowing after you make it. Everything will be different after that defining moment. Another question that comes up is, is it time for the end? Everyone will face death, is it better to do it now by your own hand, or do I have things that I can learn, experience, and grow from. Is there a purpose to my existence beyond this moment. Is this my path, are there others in my life I will meet, to be around for? How will it effect others around me? Is life for me or against me? The next question is what if death isn't the end of things or if it isn't what will life be like? I'm not really sure how important questions are to a suicidal mind, it just wants what it wants.

Death is usually connected to God or a religion, so therefore it makes it a sensitive area interconnected by beliefs, traditions, hopes and faith. There are so many different sets of beliefs and variations of the same belief systems. What fits one person, doesn't always fit the belief's of another. Trying to fit everything into one mold or to satisfy every belief system into one dogma is pretty impossible because people are at different places of understanding, perceptions and needs of life. Most of it is still unknown to those in this world, beside what is. There are some who say they can connect to the "invisible" or the beyond in the world of psychics. I can't say my message would be communicating with the dead, but recognizing the possibility that life might continue after what are senses perceive as death. I think most people communicate toward the dead, whether it is just taking time to think and remember them. Talking to them in our time, or thinking of the influence of how they affect us in the present. The other connection is through religion, tradition and culture. In most of these there is a belief that life continues in some way. I think most people in general, belief or hope that life continues in some way. Most religions are based on that concept,that there is another part of life after we leave this earth. That we have a physical part to our being and a spiritual part which are our souls. That life is not just an endless cycle of bodies dying. Christianity is based on being "Saved". I've researched some in both areas, the religion part and the psychic part of looking for answers to what death means. Some people are comfortable in finding their answers through their own religion, some people I've found are open to both. The modern structure and traditions of religion and church are there to gift comfort and a source if needed. Beliefs are vast and diverse, so what feels right to one person may not feel right to another. The overall concept is for a suicidal person to stop and think what death is before the final leap. Death for certain is an end to a physical body. Beyond that is the unknown, but there are thoughts, experiences, and hopes that life does continue, this is what my story is about. The belief that if there is life after the end of a physical body, it isn't a void of thought, feelings, emotions, memory, sadness, joy and happiness.

This is one example or version of what happens regarding suicide and the afterlife from a website called Afterlife 101. People have different ideas or vague ideas of what happens, or don't really think about, until it is encountered by themselves, or affected deeply by a love one loss. Those troubled souls who are living on earth who choose to end their problems much too soon in life through suicide obviously have a very dark energy of their own they have created. Now there are many different reasons for suicide. The first we would say is that this individuals connection with it's spirit self is so blocked with negative energy that they have shut down from their spirit self. This individual is in such pain and is so confused and the wall of pain and confusion has built so strongly around him or her that the individual has closed down so much they cannot allow any love into their life.

By doing this they are looking at such a helpless and hopelessness feeling, a feeling of being totally alienated from the entire universe, feeling no sense of love whatsoever. When they commit this act of suicide they do not go to hell as many people say they do but they are in a place darker than in the place of an individual crossing over for any other reason. For this is their place of darkness that they have created. These individual souls are initially met by angels and guides and they can see the brightness and the light and love of these guides permeate so the life of the individual who committed suicide are not left in a dim world compared to where they would have been under other circumstances. They are eventually met by loved ones who have crossed over who are very glad to see them so they are living in this place of fear. Unfortunately their interaction with these loved ones is not as prolonged, through again time is not any essence whatsoever when crossing over. But they are not given opportunity at this time to move immediately into this loving family environment. They are greeted by loved ones and supported and they have been released from the majority of the torment they were experiencing upon earth. Oftentimes their immediate sense of guilt of what they have done to themselves and to their loved ones retain them in a placed such as a continuation of a school room that you might relate to as in heaven. They are looking for forgiveness from their loved ones for what they have done to them, not what they have done to themselves, but what they have done to their loved ones that their sense of guilt is again as strong as their fears that sent them to commit suicide. Their sense of guilt often prevents them from moving on for what we on earth would consider a great length of time. As they continue their spirit life, they are given opportunities to look back at their earth life they had just ended. They are given opportunities to then be open to see the love and caring of the ones that they left behind had for them. Their lack of any right to have love in their life is what drove them to commit suicide to begin with.

So as they look back upon earth on the life they had on what brought them there, whether it was shame or guilt or fear or even anger, they see how their death affects all of those surrounding them. Oftentimes those left on earth play a role in helping an individual move forward so that they can connect again with their level of spirit energy not associated with their having committed to suicide. These spirits who have committed suicide are given opportunity after opportunity to release what has brought them there so that they can move forward into their normal spirit life again. Until they can find that they can release what brought them there and know that all they have to do is say yes, I am willing to let go, I am willing to feel my rightful place that I didn't experience on earth but can move back into heaven. It is their free choice. They are oftentimes unable to accept that all they have to do is simply say yes and move forward, that they are restrained within the feelings and emotions that took them to commit suicide and do not allow themselves to move forward even in the spiritual world.

A majority of the time all spirits who have committed suicide move into their rightful place in the spirit world for they are able to see how much love is sent to them, both from those on earth and from those spirits who have come before them who are willing to say, yes I deserve this. Regardless of what they did, they are able to move into rightful journey of their spirit self. For in this place where they initially come after having committed suicide they are immediately given the opportunity to see the love and agree that they deserve this love and be willing to move into it. They are given free choice and often times the burdens that they felt upon earth are so strong that they are seeking the freedom from guilt, from the forgiveness of the loved ones on earth. They move forward once they are able to agree that they do not need to continue to carry the burden of what brought them to heaven before their designated time. They usually don't move into, shall we say, their place of origination in heaven immediately unless they have immediately allowed themselves to be released from what brought them there. Heaven gives you choices the same as earth does. Those who remain in this place they came from through suicide are many times souls who just cannot accept they have the choice and the responsibility as spirits as well as humans to move forward and therefore their growth spiritually remains where it is.

They eventually come to a place where there is love and there is forgiveness but they choose not to move beyond the place where they are and are souls that no longer move forward because that is their choice. This generally does not happen but all souls are given the choice whether to move forward or not. If they remain in this state of not choosing to move forward they have an energy that is in which you on earth would call a holding cell of suicidal individuals, and move forward into a group of spirit souls who at the level of consciousness they are. There comes a time when you make the choice to move forward that you honestly look at yourself and give yourself the love and the forgiveness. And once this happens you are able to move to the place in heaven where you would have been at the time of that evolution. This concept of not being able to love or accept yourself can happen whether here or the hereafter.

Don't Stop Fleetwood Mac

If you wake up and don't want to smile,

My sign is this song. We all have certain signs or remembrances of memory that reminds us they are right there with us when need or just that awareness that when we feel alone with sadness we are always supported if we allow it. I hear this song at just at the right time, so it has meaning outside of the verses.

I wish you well along whatever journey you find yourself in, whether it will be completely blank for you, or it will be colored with life. At the end life will continue. It's really about life not death. To enjoy the moments of the day when they come.

www.ingramcontent.com/pod-product-compliance
Lightning Source LLC
Chambersburg PA
CBHW020238290526
45784CB00003B/1027